HARD
HAT
AREA

Oh, the doors you will open!

HARCOURT SCHOOL PUBLISHERS

STORYtown

Breaking New Ground

Senior Authors
Isabel L. Beck • Roger C. Farr • Dorothy S. Strickland

Authors
Alma Flor Ada • Roxanne F. Hudson • Margaret G. McKeown
Robin C. Scarcella • Julie A. Washington

Consultants
F. Isabel Campoy • Tyrone C. Howard • David A. Monti

HOUGHTON
MIFFLIN
HARCOURT
School Publishers

HARCOURT SCHOOL PUBLISHERS

STORYtown

Breaking New Ground

HOUGHTON
MIFFLIN
HARCOURT
School Publishers

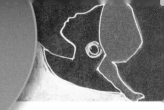

Theme 4
Tales to Tell

Contents

Theme 5
A Place for All

Contents

Theme 6
Discoveries

Contents

Comprehension Strategies

Strategies for Reading

A **strategy** is a plan for doing something well. You may use strategies before, during, and after reading.

Before You Read

- **Preview the text** by looking at the title, headings, and photographs or art.
- **Access prior knowledge** by thinking about what you already know.
- **Predict** what the text will be about and what you might learn from it. Then **set a purpose** for reading.

While You Read

Think about what you understand and do not understand. Use the comprehension strategies on page 11 to help you read and understand.

After You Read

Talk with a classmate about which strategies you used and why you used them.

Strategies to Use During Reading

- **Use Story Structure** Keep track of the characters, setting, and plot events to help you understand a story.

- **Summarize** Pause as you read to think about the most important ideas in the text.

- **Ask and Answer Questions** Ask yourself and others questions about what you read. Answer questions your teacher asks to better understand.

- **Use Graphic Organizers** Use charts and diagrams to help you read.

- **Monitor Comprehension** When you do not understand what you read, use one of these fix-up strategies.

  - **Reread**   • **Adjust Reading Rate**
  - **Read Ahead**   • **Self-Correct**

12

Theme (4) Tales to Tell

Caribbean Dancers, Monica Stewart

13

Big Idea

Characters in a fairy tale can be compared with and contrasted to real life characters.

Enduring Understanding

Clue words such as *same, both, like, however, unlike,* and *but* are used when comparing and contrasting.

Essential Question

How does a reader use clue words to compare and contrast the characters?

Spelling Words

Words with
r-Controlled Vowels
/ôr/*or, ore, our, oar, ar*

coarse	bore
warm	sport
soar	glory
wore	force
swarm	course
form	before
story	fourth
warn	

Challenge

explorer	fourteen
forest	seashore
scoreboard	

Fluency

Accuracy

Robust Vocabulary

charming
racket
tender
delighted
brittle
embraced
cunning
disguised
ingenious
outwit

Comprehension

 Compare and Contrast

 Monitor Comprehension: Read Ahead

Phonics

Words with
r-Controlled Vowels
/ôr/*or, ore, our, oar, ar*

Writing

• Character Sketch
• Conventions

Lesson 16

Lon Po Po

A RED-RIDING HOOD STORY FR

Abuelita's Lap

by Pat Mora
illustrated by Luis Vázquez

Genre: Poetry

15

Focus Skill

🌀 Compare and Contrast

When you **compare,** you tell how two things are alike. When you **contrast,** you tell how two things are different.

- Clue words that signal that two things are alike include *same, both, similar, like,* and *as well as.*
- Clue words that signal that two things are different include *however, unlike,* and *but.*

Thinking about how characters, settings, and events are alike and different can help you better understand what you are reading.

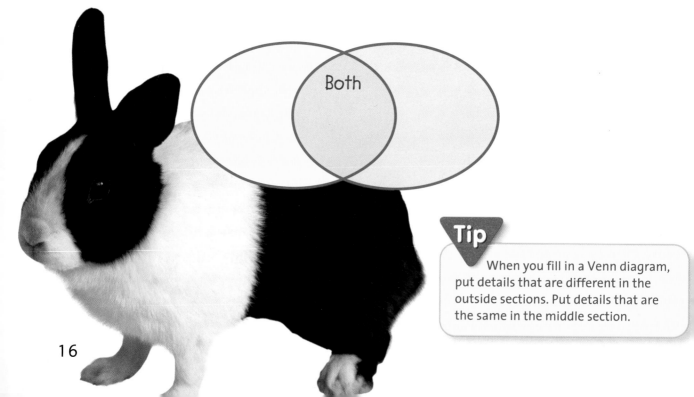

Both

Tip

When you fill in a Venn diagram, put details that are different in the outside sections. Put details that are the same in the middle section.

16

Read the story. The Venn diagram shows how Rabbit and Tortoise are alike. Use the diagram to help you tell how they are different.

Rabbit bragged all the time about how fast he was. The animals got tired of hearing him brag, especially Tortoise. One day, Tortoise decided to race Rabbit.

Dog blew a whistle, and the race began. Soon Rabbit was far ahead, so he stopped to nap in the sun. Tortoise quietly passed him. Tortoise did not stop until he reached the finish line. Rabbit woke up and ran to the finish line too late. Tortoise said, "Slow and steady wins the race!"

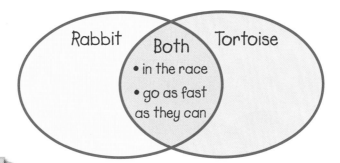

Rabbit   Both   Tortoise
• in the race
• go as fast as they can

Try This!

In which part of the Venn diagram would you write *finished the race first*?

www.harcourtschool.com/storytown

Vocabulary

tender

delighted

brittle

embraced

cunning

disguised

My Trip to Granny's House

Yesterday, I got ready to go to Granny's house. I packed a basket with muffins, some **tender** chicken, and fresh fruit. I knew that Granny would be **delighted** to see me. Granny doesn't go out too often. She says her bones feel **brittle**.

Mother **embraced** me before I went to sleep. She said, "Tomorrow, you should go through the woods. It's the fastest way. Stay on the path, and you'll be safe."

This morning, I met a wolf on the path. The wolf said he would take my basket to Granny's, but I said, "No, thank you."

Later, I found out that the wolf was **cunning**. He ran to Granny's house, hid Granny in the closet, and **disguised** himself as Granny. The wolf planned to eat me, but a woodsman saved Granny and me. It was quite a day!

GO online www.harcourtschool.com/storytown

Word Scribe

 Your mission this week is to use Vocabulary Words in your writing. For example, you could write a story about a boy who was disguised as someone else. Write in your vocabulary journal the sentences that have Vocabulary Words in them.

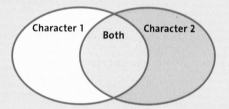

Fairy Tale

Genre Study

A **fairy tale** is a story that takes place in a make-believe world. Look for

- a character who tries to outsmart children.

- a character who is clever and courageous.

| Character 1 | Both | Character 2 |

Comprehension Strategy

Monitor comprehension—Read ahead if you do not understand something in a selection. When you have more information, the meaning may be clearer.

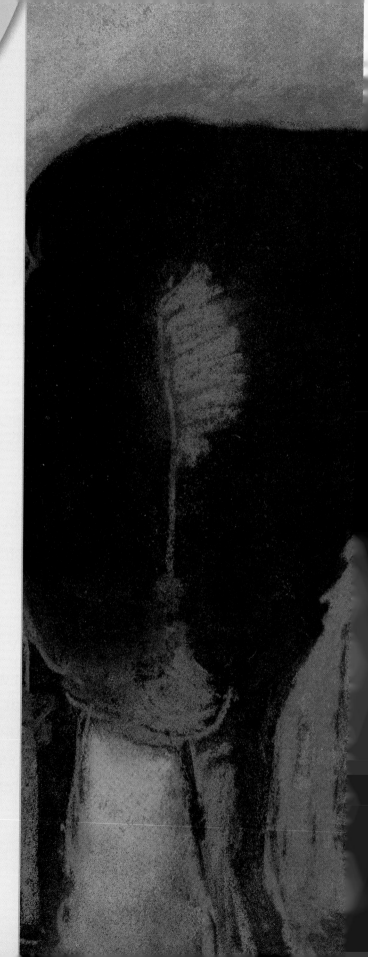

20

LonPoPo

A RED-RIDING HOOD STORY FROM CHINA

TRANSLATED AND ILLUSTRATED BY ED YOUNG

Once, long ago, there was a woman who lived alone in the country with her three children, Shang, Tao, and Paotze. On the day of their grandmother's birthday, the good mother set off to see her, leaving the three children at home.

Before she left, she said, "Be good while I am away, my heart-loving children; I will not return tonight. Remember to close the door tight at sunset and latch it well."

But an old wolf lived nearby and saw the good mother leave. At dusk, disguised as an old woman, he came up to the house of the children and knocked on the door twice: bang, bang.

Shang, who was the eldest, said through the latched door, "Who is it?"

"My little jewels," said the wolf, "this is your grandmother, your Po Po."

"Po Po!" Shang said. "Our mother has gone to visit you!"

The wolf acted surprised. "To visit me? I have not met her along the way. She must have taken a different route."

"Po Po!" Shang said. "How is it that you come so late?"

The wolf answered, "The journey is long, my children, and the day is short."

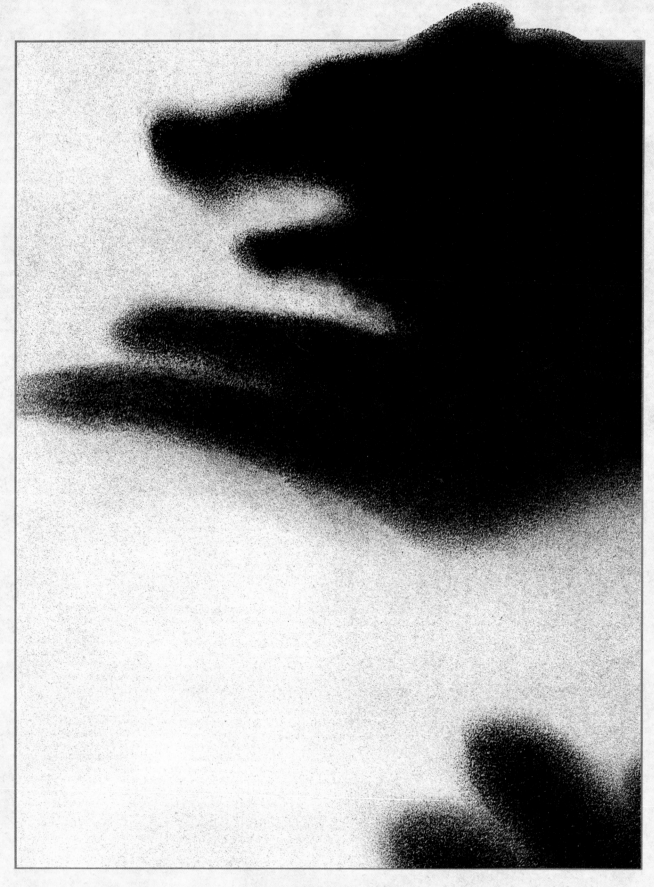

Shang listened through the door. "Po Po," she said, "why is your voice so low?"

"Your grandmother has caught a cold, good children, and it is dark and windy out here. Quickly open up, and let your Po Po come in," the cunning wolf said.

Tao and Paotze could not wait. One unlatched the door and the other opened it. They shouted, "Po Po, Po Po, come in!"

At the moment he entered the door, the wolf blew out the candle.

"Po Po," Shang asked, "why did you blow out the candle? The room is now dark."

The wolf did not answer.

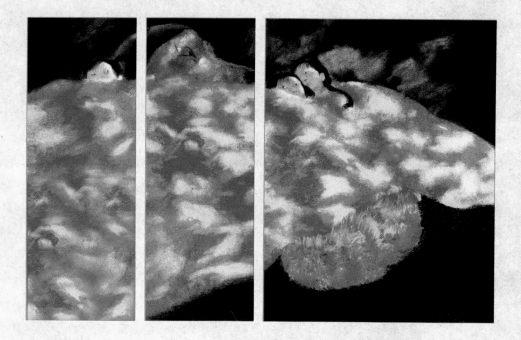

Tao and Paotze rushed to their Po Po and wished to
be hugged. The old wolf held Tao. "Good child, you are
so plump." He embraced Paotze. "Good child, you have
grown to be so sweet."

Soon the old wolf pretended to be sleepy. He yawned.
"All the chicks are in the coop," he said. "Po Po is sleepy
too." When he climbed into the big bed, Paotze climbed
in at one end with the wolf, and Shang and Tao climbed in
at the other.

But when Shang stretched, she touched the wolf's tail.
"Po Po, Po Po, your foot has a bush on it."

"Po Po has brought hemp strings to weave you a
basket," the wolf said.

Shang touched grandmother's sharp claws. "Po Po,
Po Po, your hand has thorns on it."

"Po Po has brought an awl to make shoes for you,"
the wolf said.

At once, Shang lit the light and the wolf blew it out again, but Shang had seen the wolf's hairy face.

"Po Po, Po Po," she said, for she was not only the eldest, she was the most clever, "you must be hungry. Have you eaten gingko nuts?"

"What is gingko?" the wolf asked.

"Gingko is soft and tender, like the skin of a baby. One taste and you will live forever," Shang said, "and the nuts grow on the top of the tree just outside the door."

The wolf gave a sigh. "Oh, dear. Po Po is old, her bones have become brittle. No longer can she climb trees."

"Good Po Po, we can pick some for you," Shang said.

The wolf was delighted.

Shang jumped out of bed and Tao and Paotze came
with her to the gingko tree. There, Shang told her sisters
about the wolf and all three climbed up the tall tree.

The wolf waited and waited. Plump Tao did not come
back. Sweet Paotze did not come back. Shang did not
come back, and no one brought any nuts from the gingko
tree. At last the wolf shouted, "Where are you, children?"

"Po Po," Shang called out, "we are on the top of the
tree eating gingko nuts."

"Good children," the wolf begged, "pluck some for me."

"But Po Po, gingko is magic only when it is plucked
directly from the tree. You must come and pluck it from
the tree yourself."

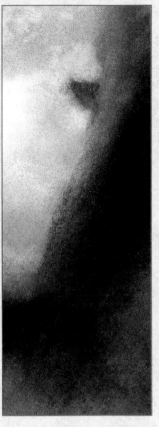

The wolf came outside and paced back and forth under the tree where he heard the three children eating the gingko nuts at the top. "Oh, Po Po, these nuts are so tasty! The skin so tender," Shang said. The wolf's mouth began to water for a taste.

Finally, Shang, the eldest and most clever child, said, "Po Po, Po Po, I have a plan. At the door there is a big basket. Behind it is a rope. Tie the rope to the basket, sit in the basket and throw the other end to me. I can pull you up."

The wolf was overjoyed and fetched the basket and the rope, then threw one end of the rope to the top of the tree. Shang caught the rope and began to pull the basket up and up.

Halfway she let go of the rope, and the basket and the wolf fell to the ground.

"I am so small and weak, Po Po," Shang pretended. "I could not hold the rope alone."

"This time I will help," Tao said. "Let us do it again."

The wolf had only one thought in his mind: to taste a gingko nut. He climbed into the basket again. Now Shang and Tao pulled the rope on the basket together, higher and higher.

Again, they let go, and again the wolf tumbled down, down, and bumped his head.

The wolf was furious. He growled and cursed. "We could not hold the rope, Po Po," Shang said, "but only one gingko nut and you will be well again."

"I shall give a hand to my sisters this time," Paotze, the youngest, said. "This time we shall not fail."

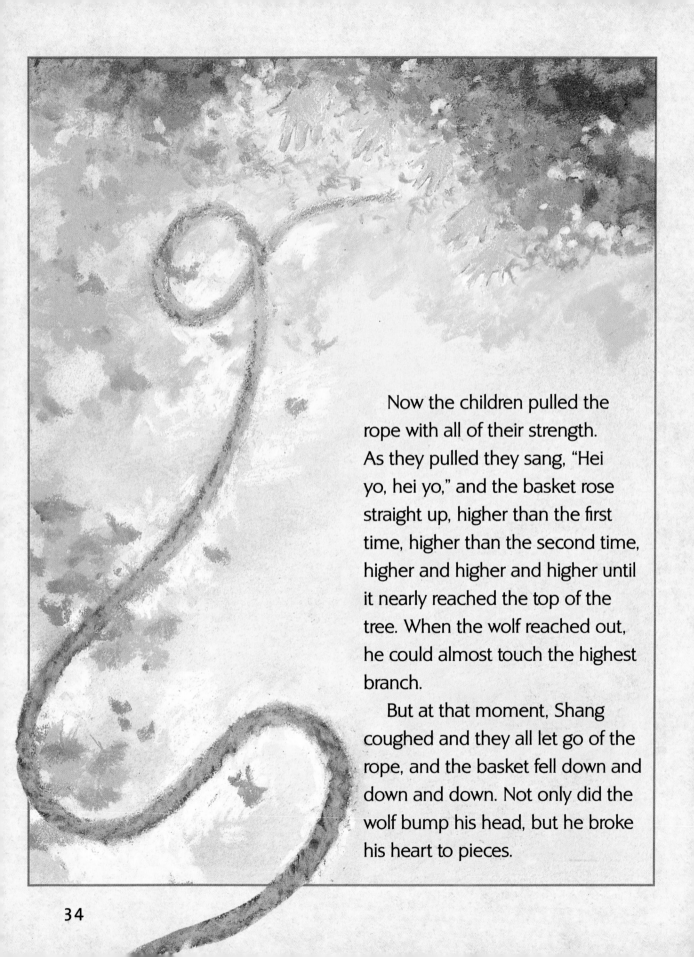

Now the children pulled the rope with all of their strength. As they pulled they sang, "Hei yo, hei yo," and the basket rose straight up, higher than the first time, higher than the second time, higher and higher and higher until it nearly reached the top of the tree. When the wolf reached out, he could almost touch the highest branch.

But at that moment, Shang coughed and they all let go of the rope, and the basket fell down and down and down. Not only did the wolf bump his head, but he broke his heart to pieces.

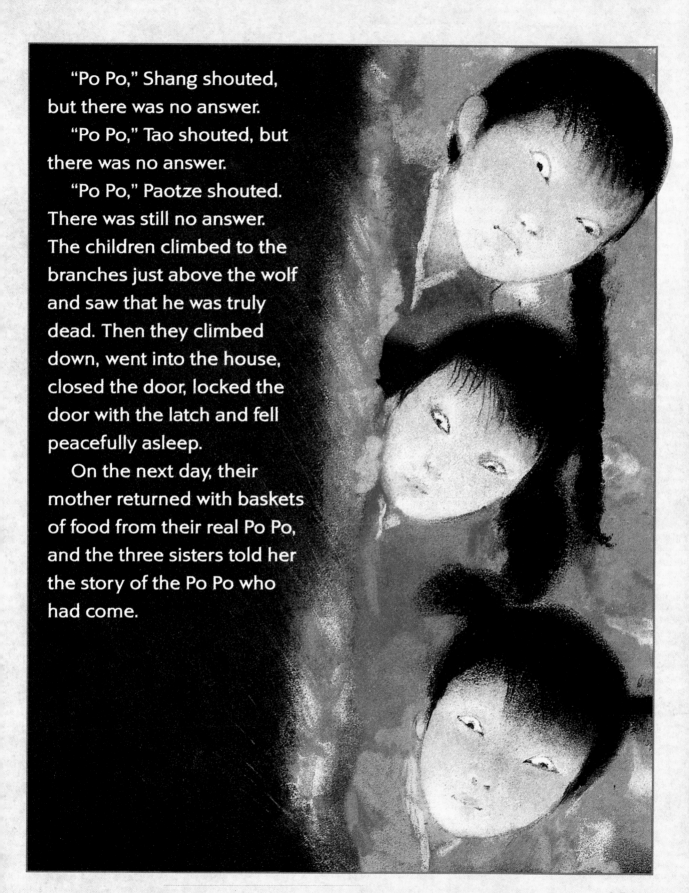

"Po Po," Shang shouted, but there was no answer.

"Po Po," Tao shouted, but there was no answer.

"Po Po," Paotze shouted. There was still no answer. The children climbed to the branches just above the wolf and saw that he was truly dead. Then they climbed down, went into the house, closed the door, locked the door with the latch and fell peacefully asleep.

On the next day, their mother returned with baskets of food from their real Po Po, and the three sisters told her the story of the Po Po who had come.

35

THINK CRITICALLY

1. How are Shang and the wolf alike? How are they different? COMPARE AND CONTRAST

2. Why does the wolf get into the basket? IMPORTANT DETAILS

3. Which story do you find more interesting, "Lon Po Po" or the read-aloud story "Little Red Riding Hood"? Why do you feel as you do? EXPRESS PERSONAL OPINIONS

4. How can you tell that the author likes the characters of Shang and her sisters better than the wolf? DRAW CONCLUSIONS

5. **WRITE** What made Shang suspicious that the visitor was not her Po Po? Use examples from the story to support your answer. SHORT RESPONSE

MEET THE AUTHOR AND ILLUSTRATOR

ED YOUNG

When he was growing up, Ed Young read anything he could find—comics, picture books, short stories, novels, detective stories, and magazines. Ed was always making up plays and creating drawings. He always knew that he would be an artist, but he had no idea he would create children's books.

Ed Young gets ideas for his books from many things, but mostly from things in nature. He goes to different places to draw, and he makes a lot of sketches. Before he made children's books, he spent a lot of time sketching animals at the Central Park Zoo in New York City.

 www.harcourtschool.com/storytown

Confetti
POEMS FOR CHILDREN

Poetry

Abuelita's Lap

by **Pat Mora**

illustrated by

Lu Vazquez

I know a place where I can sit
and tell about my day,
tell every color that I saw
from green to cactus gray.

I know a place where I can sit
and hear a favorite beat,
her heart and *cuentos* from the past,
the rhythms honey-sweet.

I know a place where I can sit
and listen to a star,
listen to its silent song
gliding from afar.

I know a place where I can sit
and hear the wind go by,
hearing it spinning round my house,
my whirling lullaby.

39

Connections

Comparing Texts

1. Compare the author's purpose of "Lon Po Po" with the author's purpose of "Abuelita's Lap."

2. What is most interesting to you about the way the girls solve their problem with the wolf?

3. How can you tell that "Lon Po Po" could not take place in real life?

Vocabulary Review

Rate a Situation

Work with a partner. Take turns reading aloud each sentence and pointing to the spot on the word line that shows how delighted or unhappy you would feel. Discuss your answers.

delighted —————————————— unhappy

- Your friend played a **cunning** trick on you.
- You ate a **tender**, juicy peach.
- You had to hold a **brittle** vase.
- You **embraced** a cactus.

tender

delighted

brittle

embraced

cunning

disguised

Fluency Practice

Readers' Theater

Meet with a group. Choose roles from "Lon Po Po," including a narrator. Practice reading a section of "Lon Po Po" as Readers' Theater. Use good expression, but concentrate on reading accurately, too. Present it to classmates, and ask for feedback.

Writing

Write a Comparison

Shang compared the wolf to her grandmother. Use a Venn diagram to show the comparisons she made. Then write a paragraph to explain how Shang knew that the wolf was disguised as her grandmother.

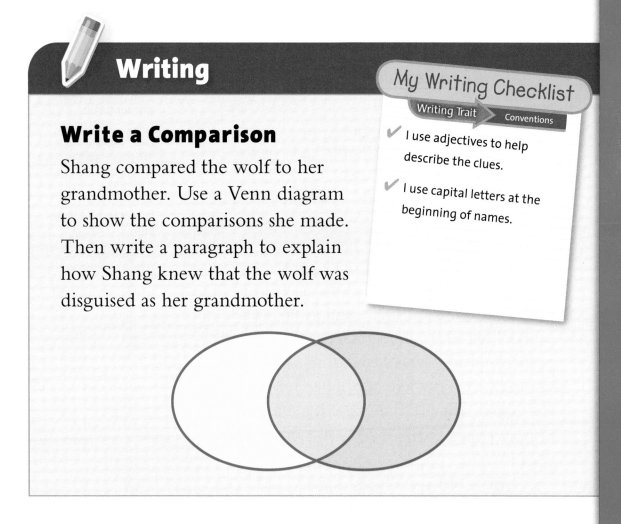

Reading-Writing Connection

Story

A **story** has a setting, characters, and a plot. It also usually has dialogue. I wrote this story after I read "Lon Po Po."

Student Writing Model

Ted Rescues a Rabbit
by Lisa

Ted and his *mom* got up early to hike in the woods. They didn't get far before Ted saw a little black rabbit under a pile of leaves.

"Look!" Ted said, "He's hurt."

"Let's get a ranger," Ted's *mom* said.

They found a ranger, who saw that one of the rabbit's legs was caught in a plastic can holder. The ranger cut the plastic off, and the rabbit limped away.

Ted and his *mother* continued hiking. At the top of the hill, they saw the rabbit hopping across the field with two smaller rabbits.

"Cool!" said Ted. "He is a she!"

Writing Trait

CONVENTIONS
Capitalize titles and proper names.

Writing Trait

VOICE
Give different characters different voices.

Here's how I write a story.

1. **I think about stories I have read. I think about the problem in each one and how it was solved.**

2. **I brainstorm story ideas of my own. I make a list or use a web.**

    Biking on Dobb's Hill
    Rescuing a rabbit
    Swimming in outer space
    Race of the giant giraffes

3. **I choose the idea I think will be most interesting to my readers.**

    Biking on Dobb's Hill
    Rescuing a rabbit
    Swimming in outer space
    Race of the giant giraffes

4. **Next, I fill in a story map to help me plan my writing.**

Characters	Setting
Ted Ted's mom ranger	woods in the morning

Plot

Problem
Ted finds an injured rabbit.

Important Events
Ted's mom gets a park ranger. The ranger saw that the rabbit's leg was caught in a can holder.

Solution
The ranger frees the rabbit from a plastic can holder.

5. **I write my story. I revise it to make it better and give it a title.**

Here is a checklist I like to use whenever I write a story. You might want to use it, too.

Checklist for Writing a Story

☐ In the beginning, I tell who the characters are and what the setting and problem are.

☐ I give each character a voice that fits him or her.

☐ In the middle, I tell how the characters try to solve the problem.

☐ I include important events that are related to the problem.

☐ I capitalize titles and proper nouns.

☐ In the ending, I tell in an interesting way how the problem is solved.

Big Idea
Graphic organizers help to compare and contrast the characters in a play.

Enduring Understanding
The reader will understand the purpose of the play by thinking about similarities and differences of the characters.

Essential Question
Why are compare-and-contrast organizational structures effective for understanding plays?

Spelling Words
Words with r-Controlled Vowels /ûr/er, ir, ur, or, ear

word	earth
girl	perfect
burn	first
work	pearl
hurt	answer
verse	person
purse	thirsty
clerk	

Challenge

creature	mixture
uncurled	return
curtain	

Fluency
Accuracy

Robust Vocabulary
- awe
- concentration
- glancing
- scolding
- console
- heroic
- drowsy
- burden
- dilemma
- commendable

Comprehension
 Compare and Contrast

 Monitor Comprehension: Read Ahead

Phonics
Words with r-Controlled Vowels /ûr/er, ir, ur, or, ear

Writing
- Play Scene
- Conventions

Lesson 17

Genre: Play

Two Bear Cubs

from a Miwok myth
adapted by Robert D. San Souci
illustrated by Tracy Walker

BRAVE MEASURING WORM

A Miwok Myth retold by
Robert D. San Souci
illustrated by Kristina Swarner

Genre: Myth

Focus Skill

Compare and Contrast

When you **compare**, you think about how things are alike. When you **contrast**, you think about how they are different. When you read a story, compare and contrast the characters, setting, and events to those in other stories you have read.

Noticing things that are alike in stories can help you make better predictions while you read. Noticing things that are different can make what you read more interesting.

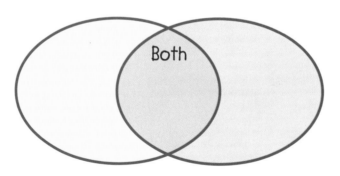

Tip
Remember to ask yourself whether the characters and setting are like or different from those in another story you have read.

Read the two story beginnings. The Venn diagram shows differences between the two settings. Think about details that show how the settings are alike.

1. Ana walked across the beach and entered the cave. Inside it was dark and cooler than the beach. She brushed up against rough walls. Once her eyes adjusted to the dark, she could see big rocks sticking up from the sandy floor. Except for the noise of the waves, she heard nothing.

2. Corey followed the path from the village to enter the rain forest. He noticed right away that it was dark and cooler than the village. When his eyes adjusted to the dark, he could see enormous tree trunks rising from the leafy floor. Birds and other animals squawked all around him!

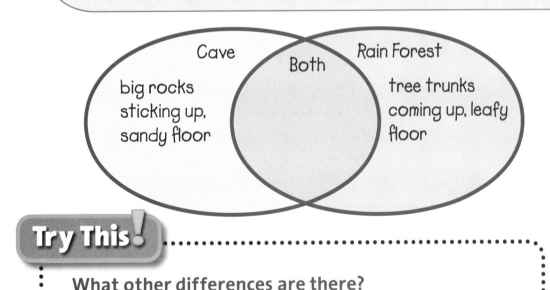

Cave — big rocks sticking up, sandy floor

Both

Rain Forest — tree trunks coming up, leafy floor

Try This!

What other differences are there?

 online www.harcourtschool.com/storytown

49

Vocabulary

glancing

scolding

console

heroic

drowsy

burden

The Miwok People

You could have learned a lot about the Miwok people of long ago by **glancing** around their villages. Some people might be making deer hides into clothing. Others might be grinding acorns to make flour.

One Miwok mother might be **scolding** her child about wasting food. Another might **console** a child who was afraid of a coyote's howl. At night, you might see people gathered around a fire, listening to a storyteller.

The Story of Fire

One of the storyteller's tales describes how the Miwok got fire. Like many such stories, it features Coyote as a **heroic** character. In the story, only Turtle has fire. He hides it underneath him and the fire doesn't harm him. One day, Coyote visits Turtle. He waits until Turtle is **drowsy** and pushes him off the fire. Coyote carries the precious **burden** of fire back to the Miwok villagers.

 GO online www.harcourtschool.com/storytown

Word Detective

Your mission this week is to look for the Vocabulary Words in folktales from Native American cultures. Each time you read a Vocabulary Word, write it in your vocabulary journal. Don't forget to tell where you found the word.

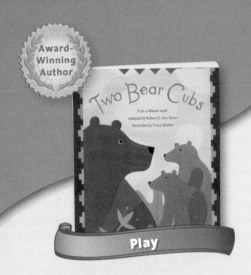

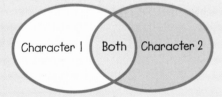
Play

Genre Study

A **play** is a story that can be performed for an audience. Look for

- parts that are read and acted out by performers.

- characters that may be alike in some ways but very different in others.

Character 1 · Both · Character 2

Comprehension Strategy

 Monitor comprehension—Read ahead for more information that may help make a story's meaning clear.

Two Bear Cubs

from a Miwok myth
adapted by Robert D. San Souci

illustrated by Tracy Walker

Characters:

STORYTELLER

MOTHER GRIZZLY

OLDER BROTHER

YOUNGER BROTHER

HAWK

FOX

BADGER

MOTHER DEER

2 FAWNS

MOUNTAIN LION

MOUSE

MEASURING WORM *(TU-TOK-A-NA)*

PROLOGUE

STORYTELLER: (*Enters from stage left*) Many snows have come and gone since this story was first told. My people, the Miwok, live in California— some in what is now called Yosemite Valley. We tell stories of the old days, when animal people lived in the valley. One story begins with MOTHER GRIZZLY going to the river to catch fish for herself and her cubs (*Exits*).

SCENE 1

SETTING: *A forest and mountain, stage left; open sky dotted with clouds, stage right. Blue cloth or painted cardboard across the front of the stage suggests a river.*

(MOTHER GRIZZLY *enters from stage left, holding a fish basket, and stands on the riverbank. Her cubs,* YOUNGER BROTHER *and* OLDER BROTHER *enter and begin to play in the "water."*)

OLDER BROTHER (*Laughing and splashing*): Don't be afraid of a little water, Younger Brother!

YOUNGER BROTHER (*Splashing back*): I'm not, Older Brother!

MOTHER GRIZZLY (*Scolding*): Children! Stop scaring away the fish, or we will have nothing to eat. Out of the water, now! (*They obey but manage a last splash or two.*) I want you to gather berries— but stay close and do not go downriver. Strange things happen there.

(**MOTHER GRIZZLY** *moves to stage left; the* **CUBS** *move to stage right, while playing and pushing each other. A berry bush appears.*)

OLDER BROTHER: Look at these berries. (*He picks and eats them greedily.*) They are so sweet. Taste them!

YOUNGER BROTHER: We should take them back to Mother. (*When* OLDER BROTHER *ignores him, the younger cub begins eating berries, too. Suddenly, he rubs his stomach.*) I have eaten too many!

OLDER BROTHER: We will bring some back later. Oh, I am full, too. (*Pointing—*) Let's see what is downriver.

YOUNGER BROTHER (*Worried*): We are not supposed to go there.

OLDER BROTHER (*Taunting, starts off*): I see only the river and trees and stones. What is there to fear?

(*After a moment's hesitation,* YOUNGER BROTHER *follows.*)

YOUNGER BROTHER (*Rubbing his eyes*): I'm tired. The hot sun and my full belly make me want to sleep.

OLDER BROTHER (*Yawning*): A nap would be good.

(*A raised platform, decorated to look like a rock, slides into view.*)

YOUNGER BROTHER (*Pointing*): See that big, flat rock. It looks so warm. Let's rest there. (*The* CUBS *lie down side-by-side, stretch, and fall asleep.*)

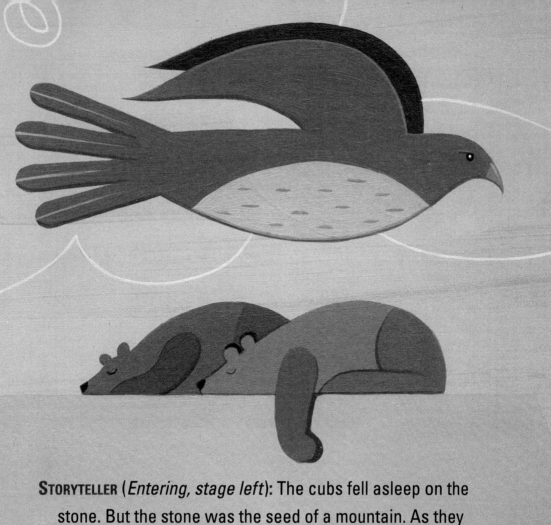

STORYTELLER (*Entering, stage left*): The cubs fell asleep on the stone. But the stone was the seed of a mountain. As they slept, the stone grew bigger and bigger, higher and higher (*His hand spiraling upward suggests the growing mountain*). It carried them so high that only HAWK saw them as he flew by (*Pauses*) . . .

(HAWK *enters, stage right, waving his arms like wings. He "flies" past the rock, looks at the sleeping* CUBS, *and then "flies" back offstage the way he came.*)

STORYTELLER (*Continuing*): . . . Meanwhile, Mother Grizzly wondered what had become of her cubs (*Exits stage left*).

SCENE 2

(FOX *and* BADGER *are onstage, leaning cedar planks against a tent-shaped frame of poles.*)

MOTHER GRIZZLY (*Enters, stage left, calling*): Older Brother! Younger Brother!

(MOTHER GRIZZLY *sees* FOX *and* BADGER.) Fox! Badger! Have you seen my cubs?

FOX: No. I have been helping Badger build a new home.

BADGER: Neither of us has seen them. We will help you look for them.

(FOX, BADGER, *and* MOTHER GRIZZLY *search to the right.* MOTHER DEER *and* FAWNS *enter, stage left, and seat themselves, grinding acorns.* FOX, BADGER, *and* MOTHER GRIZZLY *return to stage left and discover* MOTHER DEER *and her two* FAWNS.)

MOTHER GRIZZLY: Mother Deer, my little ones are missing. Have you seen them?

MOTHER DEER: They have not come by while my children and I were grinding acorns. But we will help you find them.

(MOTHER DEER *and* FAWNS *rise and join the others as they move, to stage right, and then back again, to left. They meet* MOUNTAIN LION, *carrying a load of firewood.*)

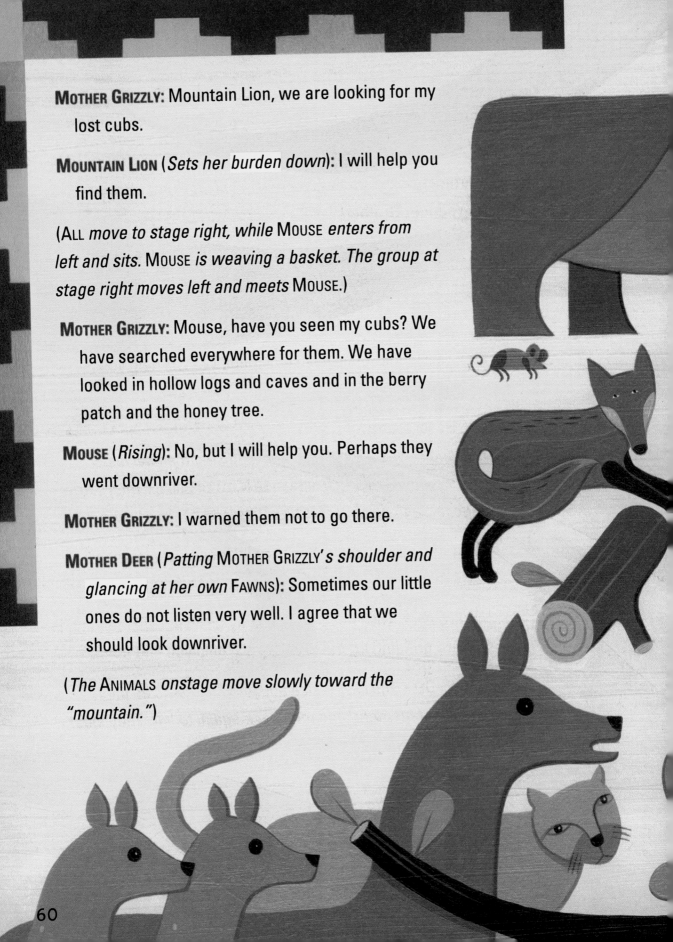

MOTHER GRIZZLY: Mountain Lion, we are looking for my lost cubs.

MOUNTAIN LION (*Sets her burden down*): I will help you find them.

(ALL *move to stage right, while* MOUSE *enters from left and sits.* MOUSE *is weaving a basket. The group at stage right moves left and meets* MOUSE.)

MOTHER GRIZZLY: Mouse, have you seen my cubs? We have searched everywhere for them. We have looked in hollow logs and caves and in the berry patch and the honey tree.

MOUSE (*Rising*): No, but I will help you. Perhaps they went downriver.

MOTHER GRIZZLY: I warned them not to go there.

MOTHER DEER (*Patting* MOTHER GRIZZLY'*s shoulder and glancing at her own* FAWNS): Sometimes our little ones do not listen very well. I agree that we should look downriver.

(*The* ANIMALS *onstage move slowly toward the "mountain."*)

Fox (*Stopping, pointing*): Look, everyone. There is a mountain where there was only a stone before.

(**All** *slowly raise their heads as they scan the mountain from base to summit. As they do,* **Hawk** *enters as before, flapping his wings.*)

Mother Grizzly: I see Hawk. (*Cups paws around her mouth and shouts "up" to* **Hawk**—) Hawk! Have you seen my lost cubs?

Hawk (*Calling "down"*): They are asleep on this strange new mountain.

Mother Grizzly (*Calling "up"*): Please fly to my children, wake them, and help them find their way down.

(HAWK *pantomimes flying toward* CUBS *and being blown back by mountain winds. After several tries, he speaks to those "below."*)

HAWK (*Calling "down"*): The wind will not let me reach your little ones. Someone will have to climb up and rescue them.

STORYTELLER (*Enters, stage left*): One by one, the animals tried to reach the cubs. (ANIMALS *pantomime their attempts as* STORYTELLER *speaks*). Mother Grizzly tried several times but always tumbled back. Mouse jumped from stone to stone but quickly got scared and jumped back down. Badger climbed a bit higher. Mother Deer, a little bit higher. Fox did even better. But none succeeded. Even Mountain Lion failed.

(*When* MOTHER GRIZZLY *sees this, she begins to weep. The other creatures gather around to console her. Unnoticed by them,* MEASURING WORM *enters.*)

MOTHER GRIZZLY (*Sadly*): Mountain Lion, you are the best climber and were my best hope. There is no one now who can save my cubs.

MEASURING WORM: I will try.

(*The other animals turn and stare at him, and then* ALL *except* MOTHER GRIZZLY *begin to laugh.*)

MOUNTAIN LION: Foolish Measuring Worm! Do you think you can do what the rest of us have failed to do?

MOUSE (*Meanly*): *Tu-tok-a-na!* Your name is longer than you are.

STORYTELLER (*Appearing stage left*): My people call Measuring Worm *Tu-tok-a-na*, which means "Little Curl-Stretch." He moves by stretching—*tu*—then curling—*tok*—the way a caterpillar moves.

MOTHER GRIZZLY (*Drying her eyes*): I welcome your help.

(MEASURING WORM *begins to climb, all the while crying,* "Tu-tok!" *The other* ANIMALS *sit, staring at the mountain, watching as the* WORM *stretches and curls in a climbing motion.*)

MEASURING WORM (*Loudly*): *Tu-tok! Tu-tok!*

SCENE 3

STORYTELLER: In time Measuring Worm climbed even higher than Mountain Lion. He climbed so high that the animals below could no longer see or hear him. Sometimes he would grow afraid and stop when he saw how high he had climbed and how much higher he had to go. Then he thought about poor Mother Grizzly so worried at the bottom of the mountain. He thought about the cubs in danger at the top. Then he found his courage again and continued to climb, all the while crying—

MEASURING WORM: *Tu-tok! Tu-tok! Tu-tok!*

(STORYTELLER *exits as* MEASURING WORM *finally crawls onto the rock. He bends over the two sleeping* CUBS *and calls—*)

MEASURING WORM: Wake up!

(*The* CUBS *are drowsy as they wake and stretch and yawn.*)

OLDER BROTHER (*Crawls and looks over the side of the "rock"*): Younger Brother! Something terrible has happened. Look how high we are.

YOUNGER BROTHER (*Also on his knees, peers down*): We are trapped here. We will never get back to our mother.

(*The* CUBS *begin to cry. They have forgotten* MEASURING WORM.)

MEASURING WORM (*Comforting the* CUBS): Do not be afraid. I have come to guide you safely down the mountain. Just follow me, and do as I say. We will follow the safe path that brought me here.

OLDER BROTHER: I am afraid I will fall.

YOUNGER BROTHER: I am scared, too.

MEASURING WORM (*Gently*): Surely Mother Grizzly's children are not so afraid, for she is the bravest creature in the valley.

OLDER BROTHER (*Puffing out his chest, and beating it with his paw*): We are grizzlies. We are brave.

YOUNGER BROTHER (*Doing same*): We will follow you.

(*They pantomime following a safe path in single file, with* MEASURING WORM *leading,* OLDER BROTHER *following, and* Younger Brother *behind. Below,* FOX *suddenly spots something, stands up, and peers more closely.*)

67

Fox (*Excitedly, pointing to a spot about halfway up the mountain*): Mother Grizzly. Look! Measuring Worm is guiding your cubs down the mountain.

(*All* ANIMALS *look where* FOX *is pointing.*)

MOTHER GRIZZLY (*Joyful, fearful*): Be careful, my children!

MOTHER DEER (*Reassuring her friend*): Trust Measuring Worm. He has brought them safely this far. He will not fail you now.

(*The* ANIMALS *continue to watch. They slowly lower their gaze to follow the climbers as they come down the mountain. At last the* CUBS *and* MEASURING WORM *make a final leap from the "mountain" to the "ground." The* CUBS *run to their mother.* MOTHER GRIZZLY *gives them a big hug. Then she pushes them away and shakes her finger at them.*)

MOTHER GRIZZLY (*Scolding*): Both of you have been very naughty! Look at the trouble and worry you have caused us all. You did not listen to me and went where you were not supposed to go!

OLDER BROTHER (*Hanging head*): I'm sorry. I won't do it again.

YOUNGER BROTHER (*Starting to cry*): I will never disobey you again.

MOTHER GRIZZLY (*Gathering them up in her arms again*): Be sure that you remember what happened today. But do not cry, little ones. It has all ended well, thanks to the help and courage of Measuring Worm.

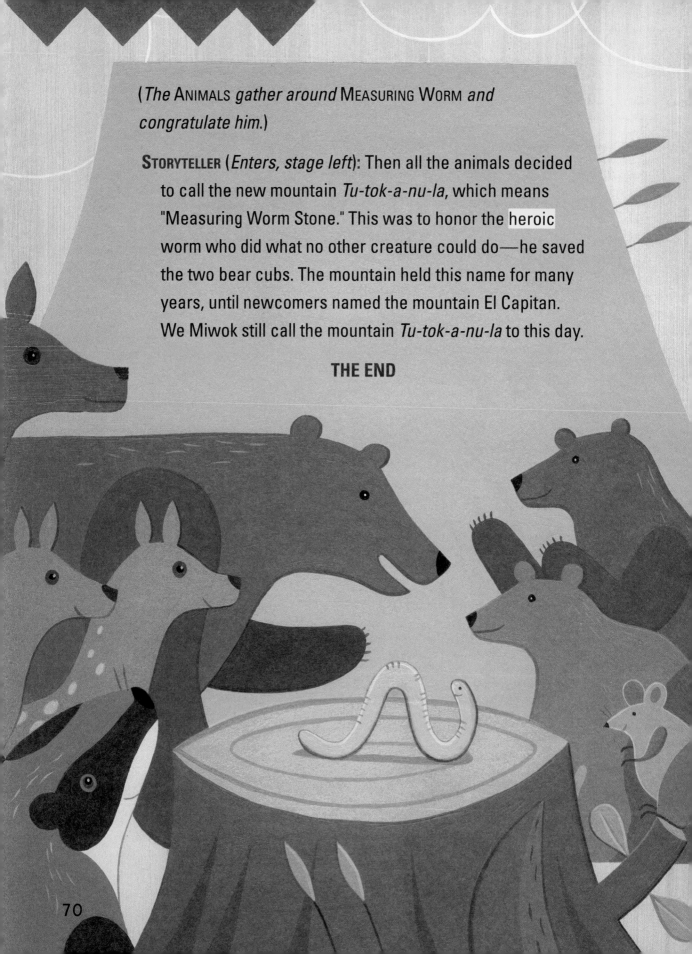

(*The* ANIMALS *gather around* MEASURING WORM *and congratulate him.*)

STORYTELLER (*Enters, stage left*): Then all the animals decided to call the new mountain *Tu-tok-a-nu-la*, which means "Measuring Worm Stone." This was to honor the heroic worm who did what no other creature could do—he saved the two bear cubs. The mountain held this name for many years, until newcomers named the mountain El Capitan. We Miwok still call the mountain *Tu-tok-a-nu-la* to this day.

THE END

Think Critically

1 How are Hawk and Measuring Worm alike and different?
 COMPARE AND CONTRAST

2 What happens to the stone after the bear cubs fall asleep on it? IMPORTANT DETAILS

3 What do you think is interesting about the characters in the story? Why do you think so? EXPRESS PERSONAL OPINIONS

4 What does this myth explain? AUTHOR'S PURPOSE

5 **WRITE** Write about a time when you did something that was hard for you. SHORT-RESPONSE

71

Meet the Playwright
Robert D. San Souci

Robert D. San Souci has loved listening to and telling stories since he was a young boy. When he was in second grade, he wrote his first book. His brother Daniel illustrated it. Then they made copies of the book and gave them to members of their family. He and his brother still work as a team on many children's books.

Most of Robert D. San Souci's ideas for books come from reading and researching. He is fascinated by folktales from around the world. His books are retellings of these tales. He hopes that through his books, young readers will discover that people around the world are alike in many ways.

Meet the Illustrator
Tracy Walker

After Tracy Walker moved from a city to a home in the country, she used her own garden to learn more about nature. She likes to study the natural forms that are around her, such as trees, plants, and flowers. She likes the designs of nature and uses these designs to inspire her art.

Do you see her love of nature in the illustrations for "Two Bear Cubs"?

Tracy Walker also likes to travel. She studies the local art wherever she goes.

GO online www.harcourtschool.com/storytown

Myth

BRAVE MEASURING —WORM—

A Miwok Myth retold by
Robert D. San Souci
illustrated by
Kristina Swarner

Once, long ago, Mother Grizzly Bear had two cubs she loved dearly. One day she went out to gather roots and berries. She took her cubs with her. The young bears ran here and there as they played. Their mother warned them, "Stay close to me."

The brothers ran on ahead, all the while racing, wrestling, and playing hide-and-seek. They forgot their mother's warning and continued further and further downriver. From a huge boulder beside the stream, they dived into the water with terrific splashes.

Weary at last, they scrambled up on the big flat rock and lay down. As the warm sunshine dried them off they fell asleep. As they dozed, the rock began to grow bigger and taller. For countless days and nights it continued to grow. The whole time, the two cubs slept on peacefully.

While the rock grew, Mother Grizzly searched for her missing cubs. In her wandering, the bear met Gray Fox, Mother Deer, Mountain Lion, and, finally, little White-Footed Mouse.

"Have you seen my cubs?" she asked each one in turn.

"No," they all said, "but we will help you search for them."

The searchers looked everywhere a cub might be. They searched in caves and in hollow logs. They looked in thickets and in the tops of trees. They found no trace.

After days of searching, the creatures finally sat together to decide what they should do next. Suddenly Red-tailed Hawk swooped down. He called to Mother Grizzly, "I have seen your cubs. They are on the granite stone, which has become a towering mountain." He continued on his way.

The bear and her friends hurried to the base of what was now a wall of rock. They called and called, but the cubs slept on.

Then, one by one, beginning with Mother Grizzly herself, the animals tried to climb the mountain. They tried and tried, but even Mountain Lion, the best climber of all, failed.

"Is there no one who can save my cubs?" asked poor Mother Grizzly.

"I will try," a small voice said. Looking down, the bear saw little Measuring Worm. The Miwok call him *Tu-tok-a-na*, which means "Little Curl-stretch." He moves as a caterpillar moves.

Most of the animals laughed at him. Even Mouse cried, "Foolish Measuring Worm! Your name is longer than you are."

Mother Grizzly picked up the tiny worm and said gratefully, "I welcome your help."

So Measuring Worm began to creep up the rock. He curled himself into an arch, anchored himself with his short back legs, and then stretched out his body until his front legs could grasp another bit of stone. As he went, he marked a safe path with a sticky thread, for Measuring Worm can make silk like a spider.

Once, Measuring Worm looked down and saw that the mighty river now seemed only a thin band of silver. The forests and meadows looked no bigger than twigs and moss. He grew afraid and could not move at all. After a time, he found his courage again. He began to sing, *Tu-tok! Tu-tok!* (which means, "Curl-stretch! Curl-stretch!") as loudly as he could, and crept still higher up the granite wall.

Finally one morning he reached the top of the vast stone. He softly whispered into the ears of the two cubs, "Wake up!"

When the cubs saw how high up they were, they began to cry. Measuring Worm comforted them. "Follow me," he said. "For I have marked a safe path with my thread."

"We are afraid we will fall," wailed the two little bears.

Measuring Worm challenged them. "Are the sons of Mother Grizzly, the bravest of animals, such cowards?" he asked.

Then, to show *Tu-tok-a-na* how brave they were, the cubs started down on their own.

"Wait!" cried the worm. "You must let me lead. There are many dangerous places where great care must be taken."

Just then, some loose gravel slipped out from under Younger Brother's paw. Older Brother grabbed him and pulled him to safety. Measuring Worm moved carefully over the loose gravel. He insisted, "You must let me go first. My thread will be our guide, but I remember what dangers lie in wait."

This time the cubs heeded him. As they made their slow, careful way down the rock wall, Measuring Worm pointed out other places where stones were loose or the edge of the path was crumbling. When they complained about sore paws and empty bellies, he promised them they would soon be safe with their mother again.

Measuring Worm even stood his ground against bad-tempered Rattlesnake, who blocked their path. The snake shook his rattle and coiled himself back as if ready to strike. The cubs were afraid, but brave Measuring Worm, small as he was, spoke loudly. "Snake, I have promised to return these cubs to Mother Grizzly. Let us by, and the creatures of the valley will know that you are a friend."

Rattlesnake, surprised by the bravery of the little worm, drew aside to let them pass. Measuring Worm thanked Rattlesnake and led the little bears on. They still had a long way to go, but the worst dangers were past.

At last the cubs and their rescuer reached the valley floor. Then how joyfully Mother Grizzly gathered her cubs to her heart and hugged them.

Then all the animals decided to call the rock *"Tu-tok-a-nu-la,"* which means "Measuring Worm Stone." This was in honor of the heroic worm, who had done what no other creature could do. The towering stone kept this name for many years, until newcomers renamed it "El Capitan."

Connections

Comparing Texts

1. Think about the bear cubs' journeys down the mountain in "Two Bear Cubs" and "Brave Measuring Worm." How are the journeys alike? How are they different?

2. How would you feel if you were Measuring Worm?

3. What did you learn from "Two Bear Cubs"?

Vocabulary Review

Word Pairs

Work with a partner. Write each Vocabulary Word on a card. Place the cards face down. Take turns flipping over two cards and writing a sentence that uses both words. Read your sentences to your partner and decide whether the Vocabulary Words are used correctly.

Glancing back, I saw the drowsy dog stopping to rest.

glancing

scolding

console

heroic

drowsy

burden

Fluency Practice

Partner Reading

Choose a section from "Two Bear Cubs" to read with a partner. Listen to each other's reading. If you make a mistake, stop to correct yourself. Practice until you can read the section without any errors.

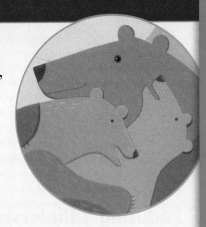

Writing

Write a Paragraph that Compares

Compare the settings of "Two Bear Cubs" and another story you have read. Write a paragraph to tell how the settings are alike. Use a Venn diagram to help you plan. Use punctuation marks that will help your readers understand what you mean.

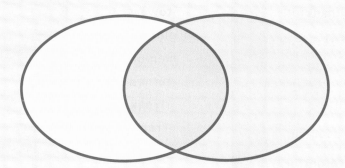

Big Idea
Historical fiction has a message,
also known as a theme.

Enduring Understanding
A story's theme, stated or unstated, is based
on the setting, the character's actions,
and the events of the story.

Essential Question
How do readers determine a story's theme?

Spelling Words

Words with Suffixes:
-er, -est, -ly, -ful

nicer	quickly
finest	careful
useful	smaller
bigger	playful
really	biggest
nicest	slowly
faster	thankful
lonely	

Challenge

finally	doubtful
gently	forgetful
delightful	

Fluency

Phrasing

Comprehension

 Theme

 Use Story
Structure

Robust Vocabulary

- dull
- towers
- glorious
- memory
- ruined
- streak
- crept
- yanked
- masterpiece
- heritage

Phonics

Words with Suffixes:
-er, -est, -ly, -ful

Writing

- Story Dialogue
- Voice

Genre: Historical Fiction

ME and UNCLE ROMIE

CLAIRE HARTFIELD
pictures by
JEROME LAGARRIGUE

THE ART OF COLLAGE

BY ASHLEY BRYAN

Genre: How-to Article

Phonics Skill

Words with -*er*, -*est*, -*ly*, and -*ful*

A suffix is a word part that is added to the end of a root word to form a new word. Look at the chart below. Think about how each suffix changes the meaning of the root word.

Word	Root Word	Suffix	New Meaning
sharper	sharp	-er	more sharp
teacher	teach	-er	one who teaches
greatest	great	-est	most great
slowly	slow	-ly	in a way that is slow
wonderful	wonder	-ful	full of wonder

You can use what you know about the meanings of suffixes to understand new words.

Tip

Sometimes the spelling of a root word changes when a suffix is added. The meaning of the root word remains the same.

Read the article below. Use the chart to tell about each underlined word, its root, its suffix, and the word's new meaning. Use a dictionary if you need help.

When Morgan and Marvin Smith were growing up in Kentucky, they were happiest making art at school. They painted with oil paints and made sculptures out of soap. As adults in the 1930s, they moved to beautiful New York City, one of the <u>biggest</u> cities in the world. The Smith brothers took pictures in Harlem, a lively African American neighborhood. Their photos show children playing games and other <u>joyful</u> scenes. They became famous <u>photographers</u>.

Word	Root Word	Suffix	Meaning

Try This!

Look back at the article. Find two more words with a suffix you learned about in this lesson. Add them to your chart.

 www.harcourtschool.com/storytown

Vocabulary

Build Robust Vocabulary

glorious

memory

ruined

streak

crept

yanked

Harlem Artists

In the 1920s and 1930s, many African American artists moved to Harlem, a part of New York City. During this time, writers, artists, and musicians created **glorious** paintings, sculptures, stories, poems, and music that are enjoyed to this day.

Palmer Hayden lived in a small town before he moved to Harlem. He used his **memory** to paint scenes of the country. He also painted scenes of lively city life in Harlem.

◀ *The Janitor Who Paints,* Palmer Hayden

Augusta Savage was born in Florida in 1892. She felt that if she stayed in her small town, her chances of success would be **ruined**. She moved to Harlem and became a famous sculptor and teacher.

Gamin, Augusta Savage

Romare Bearden grew up in New York City. Bright colors **streak** across many of his collages. He loved jazz and blues music. In one of his collages, Romare Bearden used bright colors to show how the music made him feel when a piano player's fingers **crept** across the keys or a trombone player **yanked** on the slide.

 www.harcourtschool.com/reading

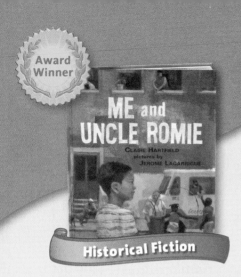

Historical Fiction

Genre Study

Historical fiction is a made-up story that is set in the past. Look for

- people and places that did exist or could have existed.

- plot events that did happen or could have happened.

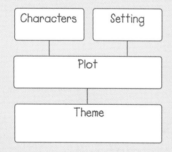

Comprehension Strategy

Use story structure to help you understand a story and its parts.

ME and UNCLE ROMIE

by Claire Hartfield

illustrated by Jerome Lagarrigue

It was the summer Mama had the twins that I first met my uncle Romie. The doctor had told Mama she had to stay off her feet till the babies got born. Daddy thought it was a good time for me to visit Uncle Romie and his wife, Aunt Nanette, up north in New York City. But I wasn't so sure. Mama had told me that Uncle Romie was some kind of artist, and he didn't have any kids. I'd seen his picture too. He looked scary—a bald-headed, fierce-eyed giant. No, I wasn't sure about this visit at all.

"Penn Station! Watch your step," the conductor said, helping me down to the platform. I did like Daddy said and found a spot for myself close to the train. Swarms of people rushed by. Soon I heard a silvery voice call my name. This had to be Aunt Nanette. I turned and saw her big smile reaching out to welcome me.

She took my hand and guided me through the rushing crowds onto an underground train called the subway. "This will take us right home," she explained.

Home was like nothing I'd ever seen before. No regular houses anywhere. Just big buildings and stores of all kinds—in the windows I saw paints, fabrics, radios, and TVs.

We turned into the corner building and climbed the stairs to the apartment—five whole flights up. *Whew!* I tried to catch my breath while Aunt Nanette flicked on the lights.

"Uncle Romie's out talking to some people about his big art show that's coming up. He'll be home soon," Aunt Nanette said. She set some milk and a plate of cookies for me on the table. "Your uncle's working very hard, so we won't see much of him for a while. His workroom—we call it his studio—is in the front of our apartment. That's where he keeps all the things he needs to make his art."

"Doesn't he just paint?" I asked.

"Uncle Romie is a collage artist," Aunt Nanette explained. "He uses paints, yes. But also photographs, newspapers, cloth. He cuts and pastes them onto a board to make his paintings."

"That sounds kinda easy," I said.

Aunt Nanette laughed.

"Well, there's a little more to it than that, James. When you see the paintings, you'll understand. Come, let's get you to bed."

Lying in the dark, I heard heavy footsteps in the hall. A giant stared at me from the doorway. "Hello there, James." Uncle Romie's voice was deep and loud, like thunder. "Thanks for the pepper jelly," he boomed. "You have a good sleep, now." Then he disappeared down the hall.

The next morning the door to Uncle Romie's studio was closed. But Aunt Nanette had plans for both of us. "Today we're going to a neighborhood called Harlem," she said. "It's where Uncle Romie lived as a boy."

Harlem was full of people walking, working, shopping, eating. Some were watching the goings-on from fire escapes. Others were sitting out on stoops greeting folks who passed by—just like the people back home calling out hellos from their front porches. Most everybody seemed to know Aunt Nanette. A lot of them asked after Uncle Romie too.

We bought peaches at the market, then stopped to visit awhile. I watched some kids playing stickball. "Go on, get in that game," Aunt Nanette said, gently pushing me over to join them. When I was all hot and sweaty, we cooled off with double chocolate scoops from the ice cream man. Later we shared some barbecue on a rooftop way up high. I felt like I was on top of the world.

As the days went by, Aunt Nanette took me all over the city—we rode a ferry boat to the Statue of Liberty . . . zoomed 102 floors up at the Empire State Building . . . window-shopped the fancy stores on Fifth Avenue . . . gobbled hot dogs in Central Park.

But it was Harlem that I liked best. I played stickball with the kids again . . . and on a really hot day a whole bunch of us ran through the icy cold water that sprayed out hard from the fire hydrant. In the evenings Aunt Nanette and I sat outside listening to the street musicians playing their saxophone songs.

On rainy days I wrote postcards and helped out around the apartment. I told Aunt Nanette about the things I liked to do back home—about baseball games, train-watching, my birthday. She told me about the special Caribbean lemon and mango cake she was going to make.

My uncle Romie stayed hidden away in his studio. But I wasn't worried anymore. Aunt Nanette would make my birthday special.

4 . . . 3 . . . 2 . . . I . . . My birthday was almost here!

And then Aunt Nanette got a phone call.

"An old aunt has died, James. I have to go away for her funeral. But don't you worry. Uncle Romie will spend your birthday with you. It'll be just fine."

That night Aunt Nanette kissed me good-bye. I knew it would not be fine at all. Uncle Romie didn't know about cakes or baseball games or anything except his dumb old paintings. My birthday was ruined.

When the sky turned black, I tucked myself into bed. I missed Mama and Daddy so much. I listened to the birds on the rooftop—their songs continued into the night.

The next morning everything was quiet. I crept out of bed and into the hall. For the first time the door to Uncle Romie's studio stood wide open. What a glorious mess! There were paints and scraps all over the floor, and around the edges were huge paintings with all sorts of pieces pasted together.

I saw saxophones, birds, fire escapes, and brown faces. *It's Harlem*, I thought. *The people, the music, the rooftops, and the stoops*. Looking at Uncle Romie's paintings, I could *feel* Harlem——its beat and bounce.

Then there was one that was different. Smaller houses, flowers, and trains. "That's home!" I shouted.

"Yep," Uncle Romie said, smiling, from the doorway. "That's the Carolina I remember."

"Mama says you visited your grandparents there most every summer when you were a kid," I said.

"I sure did, James. *Mmm*. Now that's the place for pepper jelly. Smeared thick on biscuits. And when Grandma wasn't looking . . . I'd sneak some on a spoon."

"Daddy and I do that too!" I told him.

We laughed together, then walked to the kitchen for a breakfast feast—eggs, bacon, grits, and biscuits.

"James, you've got me remembering the pepper jelly lady. People used to line up down the block to buy her preserves."

"Could you put someone like that in one of your paintings?" I asked.

"I guess I could." Uncle Romie nodded. "Yes, that's a memory just right for sharing. What a good idea, James. Now let's get this birthday going!"

He brought out two presents from home. I tore into the packages while he got down the pepper jelly and two huge spoons. Mama and Daddy had picked out just what I wanted—a special case for my baseball cards, and a model train for me to build.

"Pretty cool," said Uncle Romie. "I used to watch the trains down in North Carolina, you know."

How funny to picture big Uncle Romie lying on his belly!

"B.J. and me, we have contests to see who can hear the trains first."

"Hey, I did that too. You know, it's a funny thing, James. People live in all sorts of different places and families. But the things we care about are pretty much the same. Like favorite foods, special songs, games, stories . . . and like birthdays." Uncle Romie held up two tickets to a baseball game!

It turns out Uncle Romie knows all about baseball—he was even a star pitcher in college. We got our mitts and set off for the game.

Way up in the bleachers, we shared a bag of peanuts, cracking the shells with our teeth and keeping our mitts ready in case a home run ball came our way. That didn't happen—but we sure had fun.

Aunt Nanette came home that night. She lit the candles and we all shared my Caribbean birthday cake.

After that, Uncle Romie had to work a lot again. But at the end of each day he let me sit with him in his studio and talk. Daddy was right. Uncle Romie is a good man.

The day of the big art show finally came. I watched the people laughing and talking, walking slowly around the room from painting to painting. I walked around myself, listening to their conversations.

"Remember our first train ride from Chicago to New York?" one lady asked her husband.

"That guitar-playing man reminds me of my uncle Joe," said another.

All these strangers talking to each other about their families and friends and special times, and all because of how my uncle Romie's paintings reminded them of these things.

Later that night Daddy called. I had a brand-new brother and sister. Daddy said they were both bald and made a lot of noise. But he sounded happy and said how they all missed me.

This time Aunt Nanette and Uncle Romie took me to the train station.

"Here's a late birthday present for you, James," Uncle Romie said, holding out a package. "Open it on the train, why don't you. It'll help pass the time on the long ride home."

I waved out the window to Uncle Romie and Aunt Nanette until I couldn't see them anymore. Then I ripped off the wrappings!

And there was my summer in New York. Bright sky in one corner, city lights at night in another. Tall buildings. Baseball ticket stubs. The label from the pepper jelly jar. And trains. One going toward the skyscrapers. Another going away.

Back home, I lay in the soft North Carolina grass. It was the first of September, almost Uncle Romie's birthday. I watched the birds streak across the sky.

Rooftop birds, I thought. *Back home from their summer in New York, just like me.* Watching them, I could still feel the city's beat inside my head.

A feather drifted down from the sky. In the garden tiger lilies bent in the wind. *Uncle Romie's favorite flowers*. I yanked off a few blossoms. And then I was off on a treasure hunt, collecting things that reminded me of Uncle Romie.

I painted and pasted them together on a big piece of cardboard. Right in the middle I put the train schedule. And at the top I wrote:

Happy Birthday
Uncle Romie

THINK CRITICALLY

1 What is the theme of "Me and Uncle Romie"? THEME

2 What does Uncle Romie give James as a present?
IMPORTANT DETAILS

3 If you were James, what would you put in a collage for Aunt Nanette? Explain your choices. EXPRESS PERSONAL OPINIONS

4 How does the author feel about New York City? How can you tell? DRAW CONCLUSIONS

5 **WRITE** How do James's feelings about his uncle change after he sees his uncle's artwork? Give examples from the story to support your answer. EXTENDED RESPONSE

Meet the Author
Claire Hartfield

As a young girl, Claire Hartfield was very shy. When she was five, she began taking dance lessons. She found that dance helped her express her ideas. She continued to dance until she was an adult.

The author got the idea for *Me and Uncle Romie* after seeing the collage art of a famous artist. The collage reminded her of dance. She says that collage art, like dance, tells stories about people's lives. Claire Hartfield enjoys visiting schools to share her story with children and help them tell their own stories.

Jerome Lagarrigue

Jerome Lagarrigue grew up in Paris, France. Every summer, he visited his grandmother in Harlem, part of New York City. Like James in *Me and Uncle Romie,* he enjoyed the sights and sounds of the city on his visits.

In addition to illustrating children's books, the artist paints and teaches painting. He likes to paint people and places that have special meaning for him. Some people say Jerome Lagarrigue's art makes them feel as if they want to pick up a brush and start painting.

 www.harcourtschool.com/storytown

109

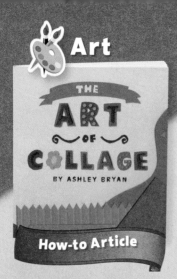

How-to Article

THE ART OF COLLAGE

BY ASHLEY BRYAN

Like Romare Bearden, I am an artist. I write and illustrate books for children. Perhaps you have seen some of my art in books you have read. An artist is not a special kind of person—every person is a special kind of artist. We can all create our own kinds of art!

Many collage artists have learned a lot from Romare Bearden. He was always trying new ways of doing things. He used many kinds of papers and added photographs, paint, and ink.

When I make a collage, I prefer to use only paper. My only tools are scissors and glue. Although there are many ways to make a collage, here is one way to do it.

from *Beautiful Blackbird* by Ashley Bryan

MAKE A COLLAGE

- pencil and scrap paper for sketching
- sheet of heavy paper or poster board
- colored papers
- scissors
- glue

DIRECTIONS

1. Think of a scene to illustrate from a story that you like.
2. Draw a sketch of what you want to show. Who are the characters, and what do they look like? What is happening in the scene?
3. Look at your sketch. What shapes need to be in the background? Choose papers for those shapes. Cut them out, and place them on the poster board. Do <u>not</u> glue anything yet.
4. Cut out your characters and other shapes. Decide how to place them in the collage. Remember that you do not have to stick to your original sketch. Until you glue down your paper shapes, you can change your mind about where to put things.
5. When you are happy with the way you have arranged your collage, glue down your paper shapes.
6. Leave your collage flat to dry. Then share your art with your classmates by telling what is happening in the scene.

Connections

Comparing Texts

1. Think about the collages Uncle Romie made and the collages Ashley Bryan makes. How are they alike and how are they different?

2. Would you like to have an aunt or uncle like the ones in the story? Explain.

3. What did you learn about New York City from the story?

Vocabulary Review

Rate a Situation

Work with a partner. Read aloud each sentence and point to the spot on the word line that shows how you would feel. Discuss your answers.

happy ———————————————— sad

- You watched as a spider **crept** across the floor.

- You had a **glorious** time at a party.

- A friend accidentally **ruined** your art project.

glorious

memory

crept

ruined

streak

yanked

Fluency Practice

Partner Reading

Work with a partner. Take turns reading aloud your favorite sections of "Me and Uncle Romie." As you read, group words into short, meaningful phrases. After you read, ask your partner for feedback.

Writing

Write a Story Plan

Write a story plan about James visiting your community. Describe the characters and the setting. Tell about the problem, important events, and solution. Be sure your story has a theme.

My Writing Checklist

Writing Trait ▶ Voice

✔ I use a story map to plan my story.

✔ I think about the change in setting and each character's voice.

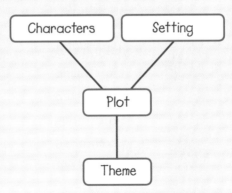

Characters — Setting

Plot

Theme

Big Idea
The theme of a folktale teaches a lesson.

Enduring Understanding
A folktale contains characters that teach a lesson through the theme and the plot.

Essential Question
How do the characters in the folktale teach a lesson?

Spelling Words
Words with Prefixes:
un-, re-, dis-

undo	remove
redo	dishonest
dislike	unhappy
react	rebuild
refill	displease
uneasy	uncover
reread	rewrite
unlike	

Challenge

recycle	unclear
disagree	disorder
review	

Fluency
Phrasing

Robust Vocabulary
- deliberately
- composed
- suggested
- enormous
- exclaimed
- swift
- vain
- overheard
- gratitude
- compassion

Comprehension
 Theme

 Use Story Structure

Phonics
Words with Prefixes:
un-, re-, dis-

Writing
- Folktale
- Voice

Lesson 19

Genre: Folktale

Genre: Folktale

CUENTO TRADICIONAL EN ESPAÑOL E INGLÉS
A FOLKTALE IN SPANISH AND ENGLISH

MEDIOPOLLITO
HALF-CHICKEN

ALMA FLOR ADA

ILUSTRADO POR • ILLUSTRATED BY
KIM HOWARD

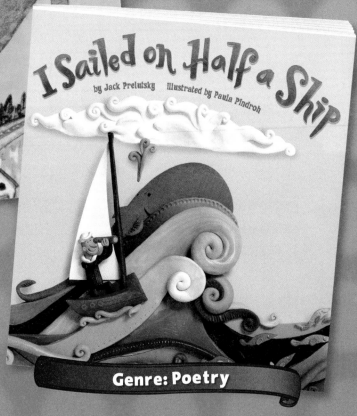

I Sailed on Half a Ship

by Jack Prelutsky   Illustrated by Paula Pindroh

Genre: Poetry

Focus Skill

🌀 Theme

Every story has characters, a setting, a plot, and a theme. The **theme** is the message of a story. It is what the author wants the reader to understand. Sometimes, the author tells you the theme. Most of the time you have to decide what the theme is, based on what happens in the story.

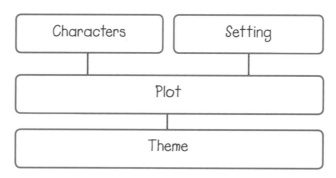

Characters	Setting
Plot	
Theme	

Tip

Think about the important events in a story. What message do they give?

Read the short story below. Use the story details to help you figure out and tell the theme of the story.

A hungry fox walked through a grove and stopped under an orange tree. High above him was a tasty orange.

He jumped and jumped, but he could not reach the orange. He turned around and saw a small rabbit watching him. Suddenly the rabbit jumped up and knocked down the orange. The rabbit started to hop away.

"Wait," said the fox. "You helped me. Let's share the orange."

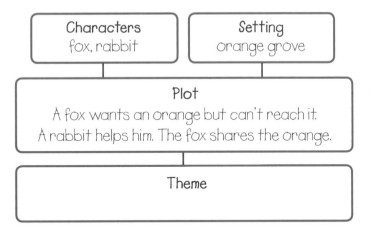

Characters fox, rabbit	Setting orange grove

Plot
A fox wants an orange but can't reach it. A rabbit helps him. The fox shares the orange.

Theme

Try This!

How would the theme change if, at the end, the fox went after the rabbit?

 www.harcourtschool.com/storytown

Vocabulary

- suggested
- enormous
- exclaimed
- swift
- vain
- overheard

Mexican Folktales

Many Mexican folktales have animal characters such as coyotes and rabbits. Here are three stories.

One night when the moon was full, Coyote met Rabbit by a pond. Rabbit **suggested** that Coyote swim out to eat an **enormous** circle of cheese floating in the pond. Coyote discovered that the "cheese" was really the reflection of the moon. "You tricked me!" Coyote **exclaimed**.

Rabbit tricked Coyote again. Coyote chased Rabbit, but **swift** Rabbit raced to the moon, where he was safe. Coyote was angry and howled at the moon. He still howls at the moon sometimes.

▲ Cuckoo

Cuckoo was very **vain** and loved her beautiful feathers. One day, she **overheard** Owl tell all the birds to collect seeds. That night, there was a fire. Cuckoo put out the fire and saved the seeds. But the fire damaged her feathers. She had nothing to be vain about anymore.

 www.harcourtschool.com/storytown

Word Detective

 Your mission this week is to look for the Vocabulary Words in folktales from the United States and other cultures. Each time you read a Vocabulary Word, write it in your vocabulary journal. Don't forget to tell where you found the word.

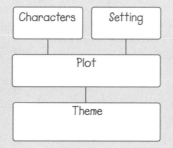

Folktale

Genre Study

A **folktale** is a story that has been passed down through time. Look for

- an explanation of how something came to be.

- a theme in the story that teaches a lesson.

Characters	Setting
Plot	
Theme	

Comprehension Strategy

Use story structure to help you follow the flow of the folktale.

120

Half-Chicken

by Alma Flor Ada
illustrated by Kim Howard

Have you ever seen a weather vane?
Do you know why there is a little rooster
on one end, spinning around to let us
know which way the wind is blowing?

Well, I'll tell you. It's an old, old story
that my grandmother once told me. And
before that, her grandmother told it to
her. It goes like this . . .

A long, long time ago, on a Mexican ranch, a mother hen was sitting on her eggs. One by one, the baby chicks began to hatch, leaving their empty shells behind. One, two, three, four . . . twelve chicks had hatched. But the last egg still had not cracked open.

The hen did not know what to do. The chicks were running here and there, and she could not chase after them because she was still sitting on the last egg.

Finally there was a tiny sound. The baby chick was pecking at its egg from the inside. The hen quickly helped it break open the shell, and at last the thirteenth chick came out into the world.

Yet this was no ordinary chick. He had only one wing, only one leg, only one eye, and only half as many feathers as the other chicks.

It was not long before everyone at the ranch knew that a very special chick had been born.

The ducks told the turkeys. The turkeys told the pigeons. The pigeons told the swallows. And the swallows flew over the fields, spreading the news to the cows grazing peacefully with their calves, the fierce bulls, and the swift horses.

Soon the hen was surrounded by animals who wanted to see the strange chicken.

One of the ducks said, "But he only has one wing!"

And one of the turkeys added, "Why, he's only a . . . half chicken!"

From then on, everyone called him Half-Chicken. And Half-Chicken, finding himself at the center of all this attention, became very vain.

One day he overheard the swallows, who traveled a great deal, talking about him: "Not even at the court of the viceroy in Mexico City is there anyone so unique."

Then Half-Chicken decided that it was time for him to leave the ranch. Early one morning he said his farewells, announcing:

"Good-bye, good-bye!
I'm off to Mexico City
to see the court of the viceroy!"

And *hip hop hip hop*, off he went, hippety-hopping along on his only foot.

Half-Chicken had not walked very far when he found a stream whose waters were blocked by some branches.

"Good morning, Half-Chicken. Would you please move the branches that are blocking my way?" asked the stream.

Half-Chicken moved the branches aside. But when the stream suggested that he stay awhile and take a swim, he answered:

*"I have no time to lose.
I'm off to Mexico City
to see the court of the viceroy!"*

And *hip hop hip hop*, off he went, hippety-hopping along on his only foot.

A little while later, Half-Chicken found a small fire burning between some rocks. The fire was almost out.

"Good morning, Half-Chicken. Please, fan me a little with your wing, for I am about to go out," asked the fire.

Half-Chicken fanned the fire with his wing, and it blazed up again. But when the fire suggested that he stay awhile and warm up, he answered:

"I have no time to lose.
I'm off to Mexico City
to see the court of the viceroy!"

And *hip hop hip hop*, off he went, hippety-hopping along on his only foot.

After he had walked a little farther, Half-Chicken found the wind tangled in some bushes.

"Good morning, Half-Chicken. Would you please untangle me, so that I can go on my way?" asked the wind.

Half-Chicken untangled the branches. But when the wind suggested that he stay and play, and offered to help him fly here and there like a dry leaf, he answered:

"I have no time to lose.
I'm off to Mexico City
to see the court of the viceroy!"

And *hip hop hip hop*, off he went, hippety-hopping along on his only foot. At last he reached Mexico City.

Half-Chicken crossed the enormous Great Plaza. He passed the stalls laden with meat, fish, vegetables, fruit, cheese, and honey. He passed the Parián, the market where all kinds of beautiful goods were sold. Finally, he reached the gate of the viceroy's palace.

"Good afternoon," said Half-Chicken to the guards in fancy uniforms who stood in front of the palace. "I've come to see the viceroy."

One of the guards began to laugh. The other one said, "You'd better go in around the back and through the kitchen."

So Half-Chicken went, *hip hop hip hop*, around the palace and to the kitchen door.

131

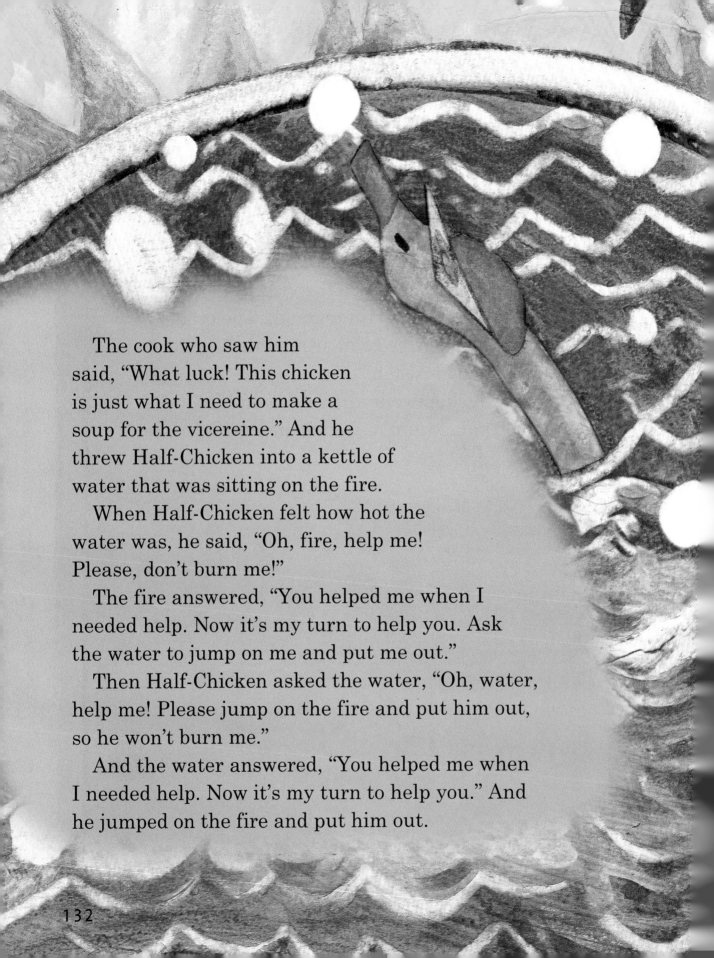

The cook who saw him said, "What luck! This chicken is just what I need to make a soup for the vicereine." And he threw Half-Chicken into a kettle of water that was sitting on the fire.

When Half-Chicken felt how hot the water was, he said, "Oh, fire, help me! Please, don't burn me!"

The fire answered, "You helped me when I needed help. Now it's my turn to help you. Ask the water to jump on me and put me out."

Then Half-Chicken asked the water, "Oh, water, help me! Please jump on the fire and put him out, so he won't burn me."

And the water answered, "You helped me when I needed help. Now it's my turn to help you." And he jumped on the fire and put him out.

When the cook returned, he saw that the water had spilled and the fire was out.

"This chicken has been more trouble than he's worth!" exclaimed the cook. "Besides, one of the ladies-in-waiting just told me that the vicereine doesn't want any soup. She wants to eat nothing but salad."

And he picked Half-Chicken up by his only leg and flung him out the window.

When Half-Chicken was tumbling through the air, he called out: "Oh, wind, help me, please!"

And the wind answered, "You helped me when I needed help. Now it's my turn to help you."

And the wind blew fiercely. He lifted Half-Chicken higher and higher, until the little rooster landed on one of the towers of the palace.

"From there you can see everything you want, Half-Chicken, with no danger of ending up in the cooking pot."

And from that day on, weathercocks have stood on their only leg, seeing everything that happens below, and pointing whichever way their friend the wind blows.

Think Critically

1. What is the theme of "Half-Chicken"? THEME

2. Where does the wind put Half-Chicken at the end of the story? IMPORTANT DETAILS

3. What do you think Half-Chicken likes best about where the wind takes him at the end of the story? Explain. EXPRESS PERSONAL OPINIONS

4. How does the author let you know that you will be reading a folktale? DRAW CONCLUSIONS

5. WRITE Half-Chicken helps a stream, a fire, and the wind. Write about a time when you helped someone. SHORT RESPONSE

Meet the Author

Alma Flor Ada

Alma Flor Ada comes from a family of storytellers. Her grandmother told folktales, her uncle told family stories, and her father told bedtime stories that taught her about history. With all these storytellers around her, it is not a surprise that she became a writer!

Alma Flor Ada's grandmother first told her the story of Half-Chicken. Now she looks for unique weather vanes wherever she goes.

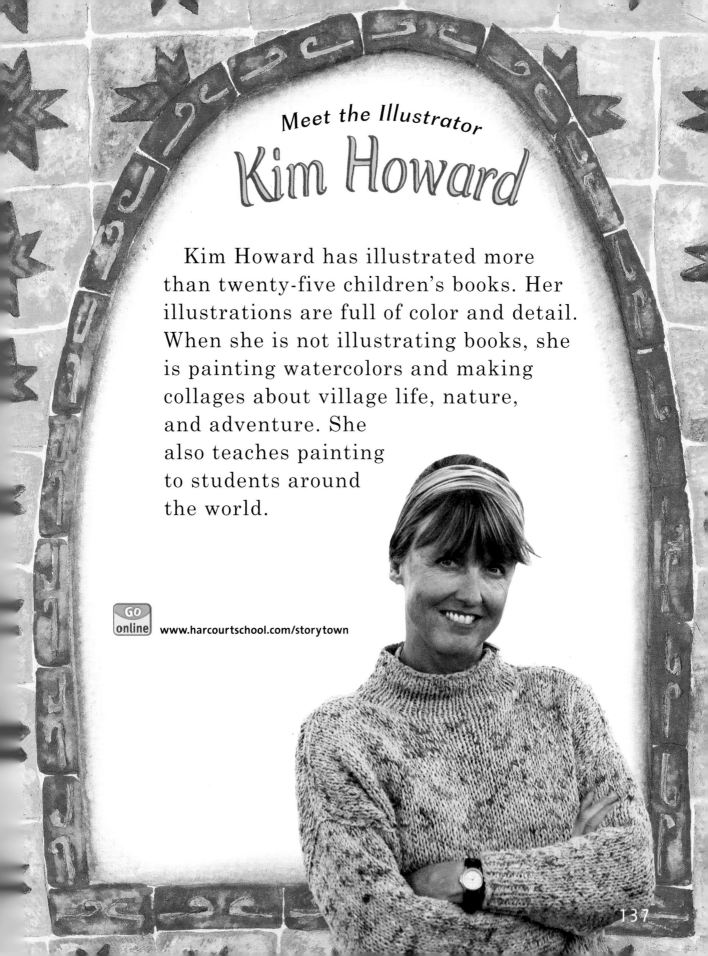

Meet the Illustrator
Kim Howard

Kim Howard has illustrated more than twenty-five children's books. Her illustrations are full of color and detail. When she is not illustrating books, she is painting watercolors and making collages about village life, nature, and adventure. She also teaches painting to students around the world.

GO online www.harcourtschool.com/storytown

137

I Sailed on

by Jack Prelutsky

Poetry

I sailed on half a ship
on half the seven seas,
propelled by half a sail
that blew in half a breeze.
I climbed up half a mast
and sighted half a whale
that rose on half a mighty wave
and flourished half a tail.

Each day, with half a hook
and half a rod and reel,
I landed half a fish
that served as half a meal.

138

Half a Ship

illustrated by Paula Pindroh

I ate off half a plate,
I drank from half a glass,
then mopped up half the starboard deck
and polished half the brass.

When half a year had passed,
as told by half a clock,
I entered half a port
and berthed at half a dock.
Since half my aunts were there
and half my uncles too,
I told them half this half-baked tale
that's half entirely true.

Connections

Comparing Texts

1. How are Half-Chicken and the narrator of "I Sailed on Half a Ship" alike and different?

2. Would you suggest this story to a friend who likes folktales? Why or why not?

3. What lesson could you learn from reading "Half-Chicken"?

Vocabulary Review

Word Webs

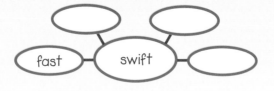

suggested

enormous

exclaimed

swift

vain

overheard

Work with a partner. Choose two Vocabulary Words. Create a word web for each word. Put the Vocabulary Word in the center of your web. Then write related words in the web. Share your webs with your partner.

Fluency Practice

Readers' Theater

Meet with a group. Choose roles from "Half-Chicken," including the narrator. Choose a section of the story to read as Readers' Theater. Group words into phrases to make your reading smooth. Ask for audience feedback.

Writing

Write a Review

Would "Half-Chicken" make a good movie? Write a review to tell why or why not. Describe the characters and setting. Summarize the problem, important events, and solution. Don't forget to include the theme.

My Writing Checklist

Writing Trait → Voice

✔ I use a story map to plan my story.

✔ I support my opinion with story details.

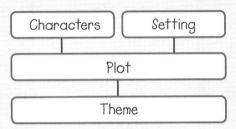

Characters | Setting

Plot

Theme

Big Idea
A Readers' Theater selection can be used to compare and contrast a theme.

Enduring Understanding
Readers use similarities and differences in a graphic organizer to understand the theme.

Essential Question
How do readers use a graphic organizer to compare and contrast?

Spelling Words

Review

form	warn
work	lonely
wore	perfect
earth	refill
fourth	girl
bigger	dishonest
soar	burn
finest	

Fluency

Review
Accuracy, Phrasing

Comprehension

Review
 Compare and Contrast, Theme

 Monitor Comprehension: Read Ahead, Use Story Structure

Robust Vocabulary

- versions
- rehearse
- mandatory
- criticize
- immerse
- dialogue
- camaraderie
- flawless
- tragic
- limp

Phonics

Review
- Words with *r*-Controlled Vowels /ôr/or, ore, our, oar, ar; /ûr/er, ir, ur, or, ear
- Words with Suffixes: -er, -est, -ly, -ful
- Words with Prefixes: un-, re-, dis-

Writing
- *Review* Conventions, Voice
- Revise and Publish

Lesson 20
Theme Review and Vocabulary Builder

Readers' Theater
INTERVIEW

BACKSTAGE
with
Chris and Casey

Reading Fiction
FABLE

THE
CRACKED
CHINESE
JUG
by Carolyn Han

versions

rehearse

mandatory

criticize

immerse

dialogue

Reading for Fluency

When you read a script aloud,

- read carefully so that you make as few mistakes as possible.

- group words that go together to make your reading sound natural.

BACKSTAGE
with
Chris and Casey

Roles

Chris	Director	Designer
Casey	Actor	Crew Leader

Setting: *Backstage in a large theater*

Chris: We are backstage at the play *Sleeping Beauty*. The play will open tonight to a sold-out audience.

Casey: We are delighted to be interviewing some of the cast and crew of *Sleeping Beauty*. We have many questions for them. Let's get started!

Chris: Welcome, Director. Would you please start by telling us what a director does?

Director: Being a director takes an enormous amount of work. My job is to put the whole show together. I have been working on *Sleeping Beauty* for almost six months. Tonight, we will perform for an audience for the first time.

Chris: How did you get started on this play?

Director: First, I chose the script. There are many versions of *Sleeping Beauty*. I chose the one that I thought told the story in the most interesting way.

Chris: What did you do after you had a script?

Director: I found actors, designers, and crew members.

Casey: Did your job become easier after you had people to help you?

Director: I hired great people, but the hard part had just begun. Putting on a play is a lot of work. We needed to rehearse every day. We have had mandatory rehearsals every day for more than two months.

Fluency Tip

When you read large sections of text, be sure not to skip over any words. Read the section to yourself before you read it aloud.

Chris: What happens at a rehearsal?

Director: The actors practice their parts again and again. Part of my job is to pay attention to their acting. Then I give them tips on how they can make the performance better.

Casey: That sounds interesting. What is the hardest part of being a director?

Director: Good question. It is difficult to criticize an actor's work. I try to do it gently. I don't want to hurt the actor's feelings. I just want to show him or her a better way to do things.

Chris: That does sound difficult.

Director: It is, but the hardest part of directing is taking a good play and making it into a great play. This takes a lot of work from everyone, especially the actors.

Chris: What does an actor do besides say lines?

Actor: I can answer this question for you. Reading and learning lines is just a small part of an actor's job.

Casey: I thought so. Please tell me more about your job.

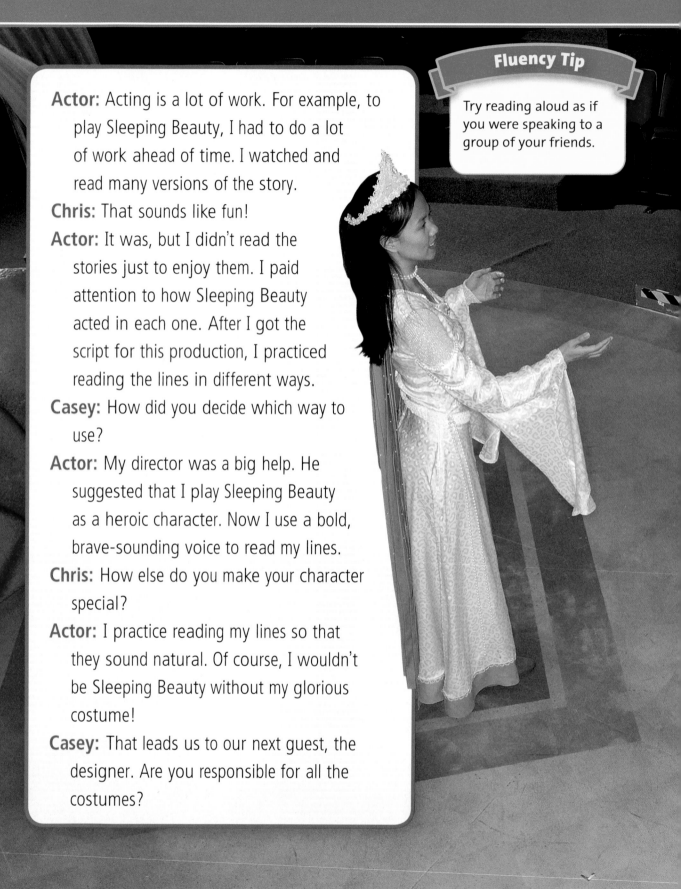

Fluency Tip

Try reading aloud as if you were speaking to a group of your friends.

Actor: Acting is a lot of work. For example, to play Sleeping Beauty, I had to do a lot of work ahead of time. I watched and read many versions of the story.

Chris: That sounds like fun!

Actor: It was, but I didn't read the stories just to enjoy them. I paid attention to how Sleeping Beauty acted in each one. After I got the script for this production, I practiced reading the lines in different ways.

Casey: How did you decide which way to use?

Actor: My director was a big help. He suggested that I play Sleeping Beauty as a heroic character. Now I use a bold, brave-sounding voice to read my lines.

Chris: How else do you make your character special?

Actor: I practice reading my lines so that they sound natural. Of course, I wouldn't be Sleeping Beauty without my glorious costume!

Casey: That leads us to our next guest, the designer. Are you responsible for all the costumes?

148

Designer: That's right. I work with a team that makes costumes for our production. I love to draw, so I really enjoy creating costumes.

Chris: Do you design anything else?

Designer: Oh, yes. I want to immerse our audience in the world of Sleeping Beauty. To do this, I design the sets to look real.

Casey: You must be very busy!

Designer: I am! I help the director with the lights, sound effects, and music. Then I work with the crew leader to make our ideas come to life.

Casey: I'm impressed. How did you learn about design?

Designer: I went to an art school. I like to read about famous artists and designers. I get ideas by going to plays and museums. I learn about design all the time just by looking at the world around me!

Chris: Crew Leader, I just heard a bit about your job from the designer.

Crew Leader: That's right. My team and I help all the people in the show do their jobs. We make sure that things go smoothly.

Casey: What are some of the jobs that you do?

Crew Leader: My biggest job is to run the soundboard. The soundboard controls all the sound in the show. I make sure that the audience can hear the dialogue and the music.

Chris: It would be hard to understand the play without your help!

Crew Leader: The amount of work isn't a burden to me. I just need to pay careful attention to what is happening onstage. I need to be able to fix any problem quickly so that the show is not ruined by a problem with the sound.

Casey: Thank you all so much for your time. I know you have a lot to do to prepare for the opening tonight.

Chris: We have one more question for each of you to answer before you go. What would you tell someone who dreams of being in your shoes one day? Crew Leader, let's start with you.

Crew Leader: Anyone who wants to be a crew leader must be able to pay attention to details and solve problems quickly.

Casey: What advice would you give, Director?

Director: A director must get along well with people. When you respect others, it is easier to work with them.

Chris: Great advice, Director. What would you say, Actor?

Actor: To become good at what I do, I had to work hard for many years. I take my job very seriously, and I practice. Anyone who wants to do my job would need to do the same.

Casey: Finally, Designer, what advice would you give?

Designer: I would tell the person to be creative. It is important to study and read about great artists. It is also important to have your own ideas and share them with the world.

Chris: Thank you again for telling about your jobs.

Casey: Good luck, and thanks for joining us backstage!

COMPREHENSION STRATEGIES
Review

Reading a Fable

Bridge to Fiction Reading Fables are brief stories that are used to teach valuable lessons. The notes on page 153 show some of the features of a fable. Scan the pages for this information each time you read a fable.

Review the Focus Strategies

You can also use the strategies you learned in this theme to help you read fables.

Monitor Comprehension—Read Ahead
If you have trouble understanding what you have read, try reading ahead. You may find information that explains what was difficult to understand.

Use Story Structure
Use what you know about how stories are arranged to help you understand what you read. Think about the characters, setting, problem, and solution of the story.

As you read "The Cracked Chinese Jug" on pages 154–155, think about where and how to use the comprehension strategies.

TITLE:
The title may give you clues about the characters and setting.

ILLUSTRATIONS:
Use the illustrations to help you understand the setting of the fable.

THE CRACKED CHINESE JUG
by Carolyn Han

Each morning Han Han fetched water for his village from the river. He placed a bamboo shoulder pole across his back and put the empty jugs on either side.

When Han Han returned to the village, he had one and a half jugs of water. One clay jug had a tiny crack, and some of its water had leaked out.

The perfect jug was proud of itself. It had carried a full load of water. But the imperfect jug was embarrassed. It had done only half of the work.

One day the cracked jug could stand it no longer. "I'm a failure," it cried. "Why do I have a crack?"

Ignoring the jug's cry, Han Han carefully filled both jugs with water at the river. By the time they reached the village, the cracked jug was again only half full. "Why don't you throw me away?" asked the broken jug.

Han Han smiled at the jugs and put them on the shelf.

The next morning when Han Han placed the jugs on the ends of his shoulder pole, he said to the broken one, "For months, I've heard you complain."

"I'm ashamed of myself," answered the cracked jug. "I'm worthless."

"Today when we return to the village, I want you to look along the path," said Han Han.

It was the first time the broken jug noticed the flowers. The colorful flowers made the cracked jug very happy. But then it remembered its crack and the leaking water, and again it felt sad.

"What did you think of the flowers?" asked Han Han.

"They're pretty," replied the jug. "They're only growing on my side of the path."

"That's right," said Han Han. "For months you've watered the wildflower seeds. Your 'failure,' as you call it, has changed our village and made it more beautiful."

"Then all that time I felt useless," said the cracked jug, "my flaw was really my most valuable part!"

BEGINNING, MIDDLE, AND END:
A fable has a clear beginning, middle and end.

MORAL:
The moral of the story is the lesson. The moral is found at the end of the story.

Apply the Strategies Read the fable "The Cracked Chinese Jug." As you read, stop and think about how you are using comprehension strategies.

THE CRACKED CHINESE JUG

by Carolyn Han

Each morning Han Han fetched water for his village from the river. He placed a bamboo shoulder pole across his back and put the empty jugs on either side.

When Han Han returned to the village, he had one and a half jugs of water. One clay jug had a tiny crack, and some of its water had leaked out.

The perfect jug was proud of itself. It had carried a full load of water. But the imperfect jug was embarrassed. It had done only half of the work.

One day the cracked jug could stand it no longer. "I'm a failure," it cried. "Why do I have a crack?"

Ignoring the jug's cry, Han Han carefully filled both jugs with water at the river. By the time they reached the village, the cracked jug was again only half full. "Why don't you throw me away?" asked the broken jug.

Han Han smiled at the jugs and put them on the shelf.

How could you use story structure to help you understand the story? Why might you read ahead?

The next morning when Han Han placed the jugs on the ends of his shoulder pole, he said to the broken one, "For months, I've heard you complain."

"I'm ashamed of myself," answered the cracked jug. "I'm worthless."

"Today when we return to the village, I want you to look along the path," said Han Han.

It was the first time the broken jug noticed the flowers. The colorful flowers made the cracked jug very happy. But then it remembered its crack and the leaking water, and again it felt sad.

"What did you think of the flowers?" asked Han Han.

"They're pretty," replied the jug. "They're only growing on my side of the path."

"That's right," said Han Han. "For months you've watered the wildflower seeds. Your 'failure,' as you call it, has changed our village and made it more beautiful."

"Then all that time I felt useless," said the cracked jug, "my flaw was really my most valuable part!"

READING-WRITING CONNECTION

Lesson 21 ▶

Lesson 22 ▶

Theme (5) A Place For All

▶ *Entrance to the Wet Dock of Bordeaux,* André Lhote

Big Idea

Expository nonfiction uses time-order events to organize the information.

Enduring Understanding

Readers use clues words *first*, *next*, *then*, and *finally* to understand the time-order events.

Essential Question

How do readers determine the time-order events in expository nonfiction?

Spelling Words

Words with /o͞o/oo, ew, ue, ui; /o͝o/oo

threw	booth
cool	school
foot	choose
cook	balloon
bruise	cartoon
hook	afternoon
tool	understood
brook	

Challenge

loosely	cookbook
cocoon	neighborhood
raccoon	

Fluency

Reading Rate

Robust Vocabulary

- conserved
- strict
- absence
- shelters
- permanently
- drifts
- scarce
- dim
- harsh
- bleak

Comprehension

 Sequence

 Monitor Comprehension: Reread

Phonics

Words with /o͞o/oo, ew, ue, ui; /o͝o/oo

Writing

- Explanation
- Sentence Fluency

Lesson 21

Jim Mastro and Norbert Wu   photographs by Norbert Wu

ANTARCTIC ICE

Diary of a Very Short Winter Day

Focus Skill

Sequence

The order in which events happen is called a **sequence**. You can follow the sequence by looking for time-order words. Words such as *first, next, then, later,* and *finally* give clues about the order in which events happen. Dates and times are also clues to sequence. Keeping track of the sequence of events helps you understand what you are reading.

First

↓

Next

↓

Then

↓

Finally

Tip

Think about what has to happen before something else can happen. This can help you figure out the sequence of events in what you read.

160

Read the article, and tell what is the next thing that happened after Shackleton sailed to Antarctica.

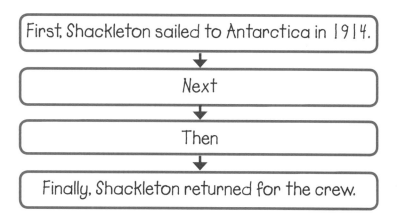

In 1914, explorer Sir Henry Shackleton sailed to Antarctica on a ship called the *Endurance*. He wanted to reach the South Pole, but the ship became trapped in the ice.

Shackleton and his crew walked about 180 miles to Elephant Island. Then Shackleton and five of the crew went by lifeboat to find help. Finally, with a rescue team, they returned to Elephant Island for the rest of the crew.

First, Shackleton sailed to Antarctica in 1914.

↓

Next

↓

Then

↓

Finally, Shackleton returned for the crew.

Try This!

Tell the next thing that happened after Shackleton and his crew became trapped.

www.harcourtschool.com/storytown

161

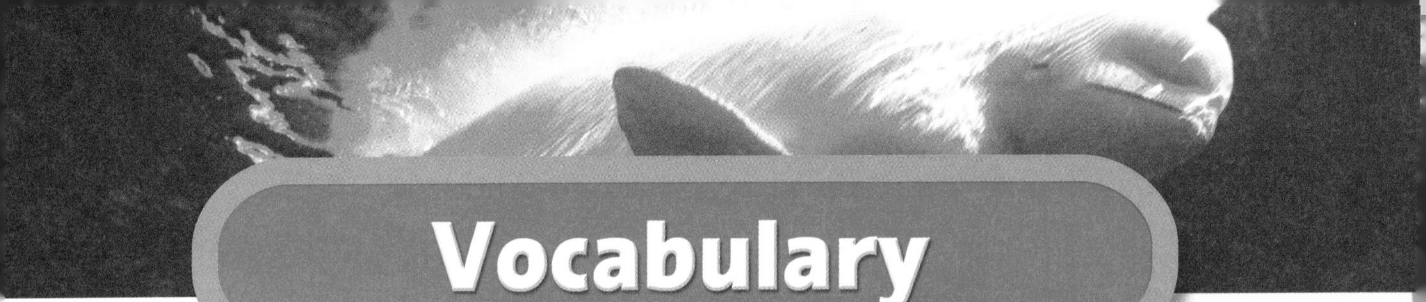

Vocabulary

Build Robust Vocabulary

- absence
- shelters
- permanently
- drifts
- scarce
- dim

Field Trip in Antarctica

Antarctica is always cold—really cold! The **absence** of the sun makes it extra hard to stay there through the dark, cold winter. Even so, scientists spend months in Antarctica to do research. The McMurdo Station **shelters** them from the worst of the cold. The scientists do not stay at the station **permanently**. When summer comes, they set out to a field camp near the ocean to do more research.

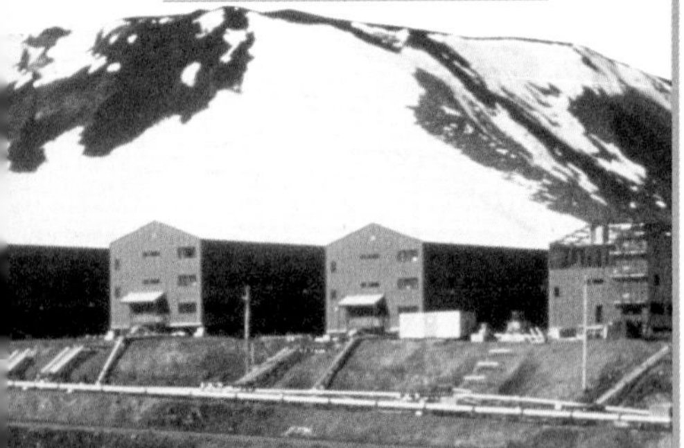

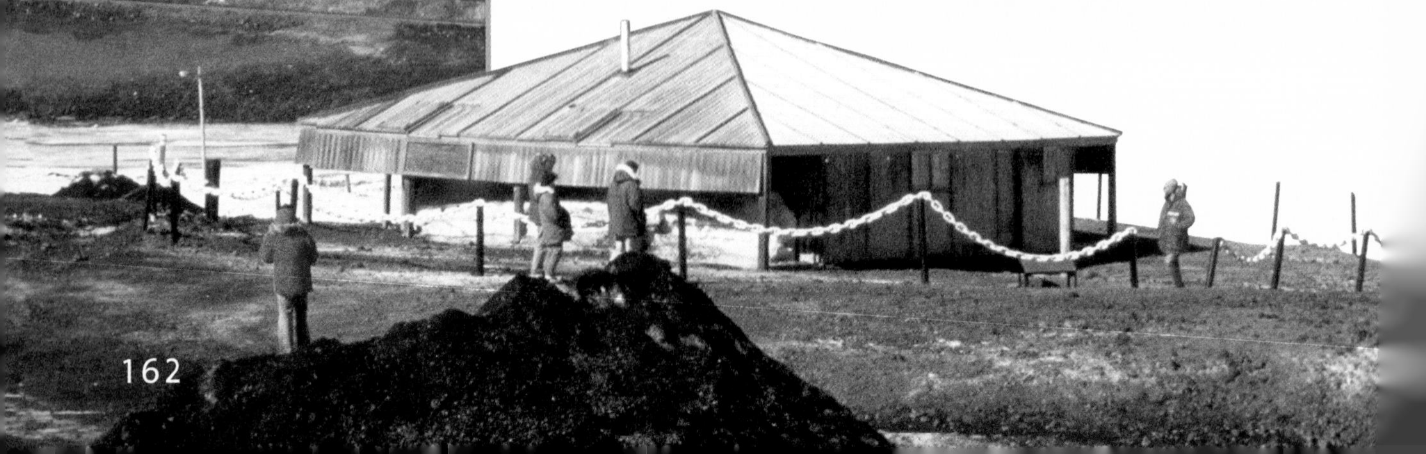

To do ocean research, the scientists must drill or blast holes in the ice. They put on special suits and dive into the cold water. They photograph amazing things, such as a sea spider as it **drifts** past.

The scientists collect samples of many sea creatures. Information about these animals and the chemicals they use to protect themselves is **scarce**. Later, the scientists will study whether the chemicals can be used in medicines.

Scientists use special cameras to film deep-sea creatures in the **dim** light.

 www.harcourtschool.com/storytown

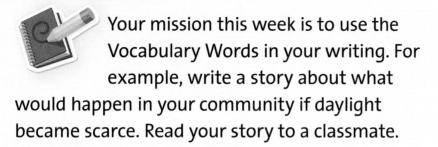

Word Scribe

Your mission this week is to use the Vocabulary Words in your writing. For example, write a story about what would happen in your community if daylight became scarce. Read your story to a classmate.

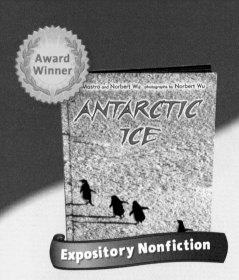

Mastro and Norbert Wu photographs by Norbert Wu

ANTARCTIC ICE

Expository Nonfiction

Genre Study

Expository nonfiction explains information and ideas. Look for

- facts and details about a topic.

- events told in time order.

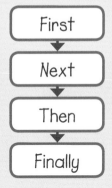

First

Next

Then

Finally

Comprehension Strategy

Monitor comprehension—reread information that doesn't make sense the first time you read it.

ANTARCTIC ICE

BY

Jim Mastro AND Norbert Wu

PHOTOGRAPHS BY

Norbert Wu

Antarctica is the coldest place on earth. Most of the mountains and valleys are permanently buried under a deep layer of ice. In winter, even the surface of the ocean freezes. There are no waves. Nothing moves except the wind.

Under the ice, animals are waiting for summer to arrive. A jellyfish drifts through the dim light. A giant sea spider crawls over the icy ocean floor. A sea star climbs the stalk of a fan worm. The worm uses its lacy tendrils to gather phytoplankton to eat.

Phytoplankton are the tiny plants that float in the ocean. Most are so small they can only be seen with a microscope. Many animals on the ocean floor eat them, but they are scarce right now. Phytoplankton need sunlight to grow, and the sun does not shine in Antarctica during the winter.

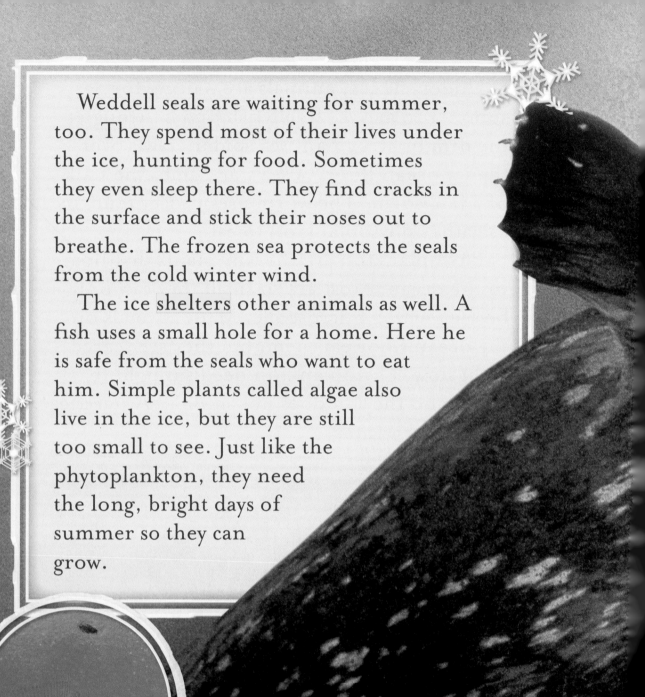

Weddell seals are waiting for summer, too. They spend most of their lives under the ice, hunting for food. Sometimes they even sleep there. They find cracks in the surface and stick their noses out to breathe. The frozen sea protects the seals from the cold winter wind.

The ice shelters other animals as well. A fish uses a small hole for a home. Here he is safe from the seals who want to eat him. Simple plants called algae also live in the ice, but they are still too small to see. Just like the phytoplankton, they need the long, bright days of summer so they can grow.

The sun returns from its long <u>absence</u>. Each day it rises higher in the sky and shines longer. Soon it is light all the time. There is no night at all. Summer has arrived in Antarctica, but it is still cold enough to keep the ocean's surface frozen.

A mother Weddell seal finds a crack in the ice and pulls herself out of the water. She inches across the frozen surface like a caterpillar. It is time for her to have a baby. The solid ice gives her a safe place to do it. When the pup arrives, he has a coat of thick fur to keep him warm.

Like the Weddell seals, emperor penguins have their babies on the sea ice. In the middle of winter, the mother penguin laid one egg. The father quickly placed it on his feet and covered it with a warm flap of skin. When the egg hatched, the baby emperor had her own movable nest. Now it is summer, and like the other chicks she has grown too big to sit on her father's feet.

An Orca whale swims over. Its breathing is very loud. *Whoosh!* The penguins can hear it from far away. The whale moves along the edge of the ice, looking for food. He can't squeeze through cracks like the Weddell seals, so he must stay near open water. Big fish live deep under the ice, and the whale hunts them. Sometimes the whale will eat seals, too, but this time they are safely out of reach on the ice.

After several days of swimming south from his winter home, an Adélie penguin arrives at the ice edge. He is on his way to the rookery, the place where he and his mate will raise their chicks. The small penguin can take only short steps, so it is a long walk for him.

At last he reaches the rookery. It is on a low hill that has no ice. The male must hurry to build his nest of stones before the female arrives. There aren't many stones around, so sometimes he sneaks over and steals one from his neighbor.

Summer is a very busy time under the ice, too. The tiny algae grow fast in the bright sun and form a brown film on the bottom of the ice. This is the food many animals have been waiting for. Urchins, sea stars, and little creatures called amphipods and krill eat the algae. Fish eat the amphipods and krill, and seals and penguins eat the fish. Penguins eat krill, too.

Back on land, the female Adélie penguin arrives at the rookery. To get reacquainted, the penguins sing to each other and wiggle their flippers. The female lays two eggs, then she leaves again. Laying has made her very hungry. She has to go back to the ocean to eat. Off she goes on her long walk over the ice. The male sits on the eggs and keeps them warm.

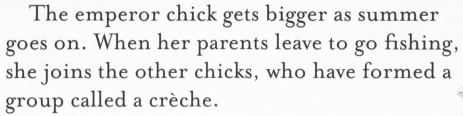

The emperor chick gets bigger as summer goes on. When her parents leave to go fishing, she joins the other chicks, who have formed a group called a crèche.

The baby emperors are still too young to swim. Without ice to stand on, they wouldn't survive. The parents come back every couple of days with their stomachs full of fish, squid, and krill. They pass some of this partially digested food into the hungry chick's mouth.

The baby Weddell seal has gotten bigger, too. His mother has decided it is time for him to learn to swim. The two of them slip through a crack into the water. The mother stays very close to protect her pup.

The sea ice softens and begins to melt in the summer sun. Large pieces break off from the edge. More and more of the sea is uncovered. The ice algae are released and drift down to the ocean floor. Sponges and other marine animals sift them out of the water to eat. Everyone depends on the algae, and the algae depend on the ice.

The female Adélie doesn't have quite as far to walk when she returns to the rookery. She replaces the father, who goes off to eat. While he is away, the eggs hatch. The two fuzzy chicks are hungry. Just like the emperor penguin parents, the mother Adélie spits up partially digested food into each chick's mouth.

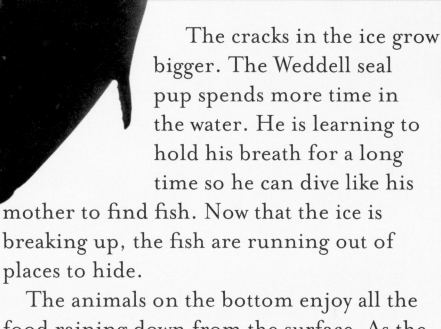

The cracks in the ice grow bigger. The Weddell seal pup spends more time in the water. He is learning to hold his breath for a long time so he can dive like his mother to find fish. Now that the ice is breaking up, the fish are running out of places to hide.

The animals on the bottom enjoy all the food raining down from the surface. As the ice breaks up, more algae fall down where they can reach it. The bright sun has made lots of phytoplankton grow in the water, and some of this drifts down to the sea floor as well. Even animals that don't eat algae and phytoplankton have a feast. Some sea stars find a nice, juicy urchin to eat.

The brief summer draws to an end. Most of the sea ice has melted. The emperor penguin chicks must quickly learn how to swim before it disappears entirely. The Adélie penguins can now just walk to the shore and jump in.

The sun dips lower in the sky. It is getting colder. The emperor chicks begin swimming north, where they will spend the winter. Once the Adélie chicks grow adult feathers, they too will dive into the ocean and swim north. In just a few days, the nests are empty.

All too soon, the short summer is over. The Orcas and Weddell seal pups have gone north for the winter, but some of the adult Weddell seals have stayed behind. They are used to living in the ice.

Winter arrives quickly in Antarctica. The ocean's surface begins to freeze again. Before long, nothing moves but the wind. Everything is waiting for summer to return once more.

Think Critically

❶ What does the father emperor penguin do after the mother penguin lays an egg? 🌀 SEQUENCE

❷ Why are algae important to the food chain? DRAW CONCLUSIONS

❸ Do you think living in Antarctica would be difficult? Why or why not? EXPRESS PERSONAL OPINIONS

❹ Which of the animals do you think the authors find most interesting? Why do you think so? AUTHORS' VIEWPOINT

❺ **WRITE** Why is summer an important season for the animals of Antarctica? Give examples to explain your answer. ✏ SHORT RESPONSE

Jim Mastro

When he was a child, Jim Mastro lived in Hawaii for three years. He loved the ocean so much that, when he got older, he studied seals and dolphins. Then one day, he saw photos of Antarctica. He knew right away that it was a place he wanted to visit.

The first time that Jim Mastro visited Antarctica, he stayed for fourteen months. He has gone back many more times. In all, he has spent more than five years there. During those visits, he made more than 250 dives beneath the sea. Jim Mastro now lives in New England with his family. Someday he hopes to return to Antarctica for another visit.

Norbert Wu

Norbert Wu had wanted to study the sea ever since he was in the second grade. That may seem odd, because he was raised far from the ocean, in Atlanta, Georgia.

Today Norbert Wu is one of the world's most famous underwater photographers. He has seen some amazing things while taking photographs under the sea. He has also been bitten by sharks, run over by an iceberg, and stung by sea wasps!

Norbert Wu's work has taken him from the freezing waters of the Antarctic to the warm Pacific. His friends say that he is always the first one in the water and the last to get out!

GO online www.harcourtschool.com/storytown

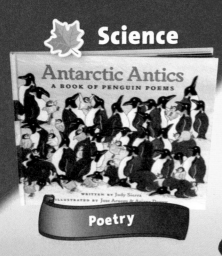

Antarctic Antics
A BOOK OF PENGUIN POEMS

WRITTEN BY Judy Sierra
ILLUSTRATED BY Jose Aruego & Ariane Dewey

Poetry

Diary of a Very Short Winter Day

by

Judy Sierra

illustrated by

Jose Aruego and Ariane Dewey

At the first hint of dawn

I awake with a yawn

And follow my cousins

(All thirty-three dozen)

To the end of the land,

Where we stand and we stand,

Playing who'll-dive-in-first,

And, fearing the worst,

We listen for seals

Who want us for meals.

I see one penguin lunge,

Then in we all plunge,

Take a bath, gulp a snack,

And climb out in a pack. . . .

Hurry back to our home

For a quick preen and comb

So our feathers aren't wet

As we watch the sun set.

Connections

Comparing Texts

1. How is the author's purpose for writing "Antarctic Ice" different from the author's purpose for writing "Diary of a Very Short Winter Day"?

2. What surprised you about Antarctica? Why?

3. What makes it difficult to survive in Antarctica?

Vocabulary Review

Rate a Situation

Work with a partner. Read aloud each sentence and point to the spot on the line that shows how you would feel. Discuss your answers.

comfortable ———————————— uncomfortable

- You are in a room with **dim** light.

- An umbrella **shelters** you from the rain.

- You lived in a desert where water was **scarce**.

absence
shelters
permanently
drifts
scarce
dim

Fluency Practice

Partner Reading

With a partner, choose a paragraph from "Antarctic Ice." Take turns reading your paragraphs to each other. Remember that when you read nonfiction, you may need to read a bit more slowly. If you make a mistake, reread the sentence correctly.

Writing

Write an Explanation

Think about what Adélie penguins do in Antarctica during the short summer. Write a paragraph that explains the sequence of events.

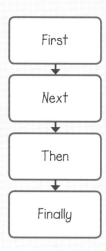

First

↓

Next

↓

Then

↓

Finally

My Writing Checklist

Writing Trait → Fluency

✔ I use a sequence chart to plan my writing.

✔ My explanation is clearly written.

✔ I use conjunctions to connect parts of my sentences.

Reading-Writing Connection

Explanation

An **explanation** tells why and how something happens. In "Antarctic Ice," penguins work together in families. I wanted to explain why and how people should do this, too.

Student Writing Model

How We All Help
by Ricardo

Why should people in families help at home? For my family, the reason is clear. My dad works days, and my mom works evenings. This means my sister and I need to help out.

When we come home from school, we do our chores. I help Mom clean up the kitchen and my sister helps Dad with dinner.

On our days off, we all ride our bikes or go swimming. Sometimes we go to the park and enjoy a picnic together. We have time for fun because we have all helped do the work at home.

Writing Trait

ORGANIZATION
A good explanation has an interesting beginning, a middle that explains why and how, and an ending that wraps things up.

Writing Trait

SENTENCE FLUENCY
Conjunctions such as *and* and *but* connect sentence ideas.

190

Here's how I write an explanation.

1. **I think about what I have read and about parts that interest me.**

2. **I use a graphic organizer to help me brainstorm. I write down my ideas about my own family.**

Helping Out at Home

Reasons for Helping	How My Family Helps
• Dad works days and Mom works evenings. • They need help!	• I help clean up the kitchen. • My sister helps Dad make dinner.

3. I look over my ideas, and I decide what to write about. I make my plan for writing.

How We All Help

Paragraph 1

Main Idea: Both of my parents work.
Details: Dad works days.
Mom works evenings.

Paragraph 2

Main Idea: My sister and I help out.
Details: I help Mom clean the kitchen. My sister helps Dad make dinner.

Paragraph 3

Main Idea: We have fun on days off.
Details: We ride our bikes.
We go swimming.
Sometimes we have a picnic.

4. I write my explanation.

Here is a checklist I like to use when I write an explanation. You can use it when you write one, too.

Checklist for Writing an Explanation

- ☐ The title gives the main idea of the whole piece.

- ☐ My explanation has main-idea sentences and detail sentences to explain *why* and *how* things happen.

- ☐ My explanation uses connections to show how my ideas are related.

- ☐ My sentences are not all the same length.

- ☐ My sentences are complete.

- ☐ I use main and helping verbs correctly. I check for correct subject-verb agreement.

Big Idea
An informational narrative gives facts about a topic.

Enduring Understanding
The sequence of events determines the organization of facts in an informational narrative.

Essential Question
How is the organization of the events in informational narrative determined?

Spelling Words

Words with /ô/o, au(gh), aw, a(l), ough

ought	cause
soft	taught
yawn	pause
walk	straw
long	false
also	author
thaw	almost
lost	

Challenge

swallow	sprawling
naughty	faucet
somersault	

Fluency

Reading Rate

Comprehension

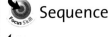 Sequence

Monitor Comprehension: Reread

Robust Vocabulary

- blanketed
- surroundings
- nocturnal
- effort
- dozes
- swoops
- detail
- fluttering
- plummet
- inverted

Phonics

Words with /ô/o, au(gh), aw, a(l), ough

Writing

- Summary
- Sentence Fluency

Lesson 22

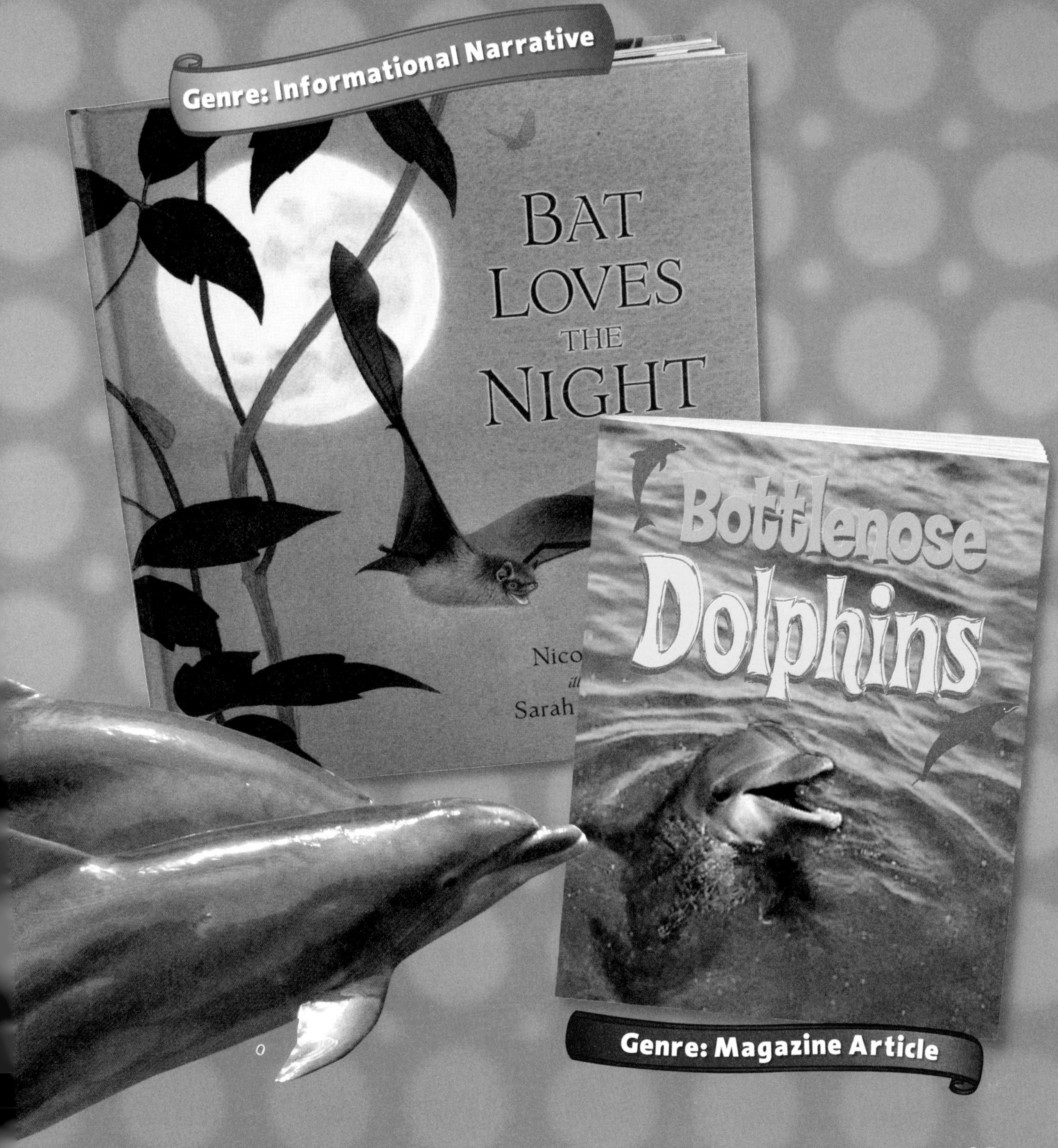

BAT
LOVES
THE
NIGHT

Nico
ill
Sarah

Bottlenose
Dolphins

Focus Skill

Sequence

Remember that **sequence** is the order in which events happen. To help you figure out the sequence, look for time-order words such as *first, next, then, later,* and *finally.* Dates and times can also help you keep track of the sequence of events.

Knowing the sequence of events can help you better understand how events are connected.

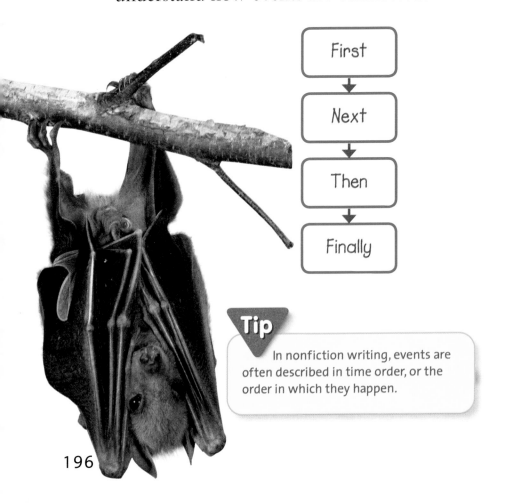

First

↓

Next

↓

Then

↓

Finally

Tip

In nonfiction writing, events are often described in time order, or the order in which they happen.

196

Read the article below. Tell how to complete the
sequence chart to show the order of events.

Egyptian fruit bats are found in
Africa and parts of Asia. They make
their homes in trees, between rocks,
and even in empty buildings.

At night the Egyptian fruit bats
fly through rainforests. They feed
on the plentiful fruits and flowers.
After they land on a flower, a powder
called pollen sticks to their bodies.
When they go to another flower, they
spread the pollen. Later, the plants use the
pollen to produce fruit.

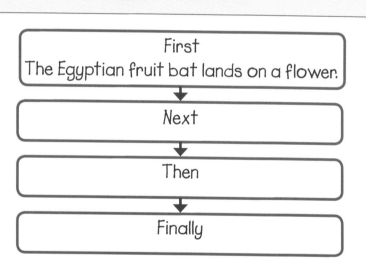

> **First**
> The Egyptian fruit bat lands on a flower.

↓

> **Next**

↓

> **Then**

↓

> **Finally**

 GO online www.harcourtschool.com/storytown

Look back at this passage. What do the bats do before
they land on flowers?

Vocabulary

Build Robust Vocabulary

nocturnal

effort

dozes

swoops

detail

fluttering

Night Flyers

Warblers and other songbirds fly by night from their summer nesting grounds to their winter feeding grounds. They make a **nocturnal** journey that takes them hundreds of miles from Canada and Alaska in North America to Venezuela and Colombia in northern South America. It takes a great **effort** to fly that distance. To keep up its strength, the bird feeds, rests, or **dozes** during the day.

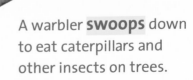

A warbler **swoops** down to eat caterpillars and other insects on trees.

The tiny songbirds must pay attention to **detail** on their journey. They use the light of the stars to help guide them. As they fly, they keep in touch with each other by singing. They do not sing full songs but make little chirps to let each other know where they are.

Blackpoll warblers may have the longest journey. Their **fluttering** wings carry them more than 14,000 miles round-trip!

The Blackpoll warbler may begin its journey in Alaska and travel as far south as Chile.

 www.harcourtschool.com/storytown

Word Detective

 Your mission this week is to look for the Vocabulary Words in science magazines or books. Each time you read a Vocabulary Word, write it in your vocabulary journal. Don't forget to tell where you found the word.

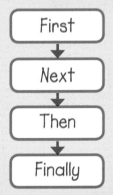

Informational Narrative

Genre Study

Informational narratives present information in the form of a story. Look for

- facts about a topic.

- events told in time order.

First

↓

Next

↓

Then

↓

Finally

Comprehension Strategy

Monitor comprehension—If you cannot figure out a word, **reread** the sentences that come before it.

BAT LOVES THE NIGHT

by Nicola Davies

illustrated by
Sarah Fox-Davies

Bat is waking,
upside down as usual,
hanging by her toenails.

Her beady eyes open.
Her pixie ears twitch.

She shakes her thistledown fur.

She unfurls her wings, made
of skin so fine the finger bones
inside show through.

The pipistrelle bat's
body is no bigger
than your thumb.

A bat's wing is its arm and hand.
Four extra-long fingers support the
skin of the wing.

Now she unhooks her toes and drops into black space. With a sound like a tiny umbrella opening, she flaps her wings.

Bat is flying.

Bats' toes are shaped like hooks, so it's no effort for a bat to hang upside down.

Out!

Out under the broken tile into the nighttime garden.

Over bushes, under trees, between fence posts, through the tangled hedge she swoops untouched. Bat is at home in the darkness as a fish is in the water. She doesn't need to see—she can hear where she is going.

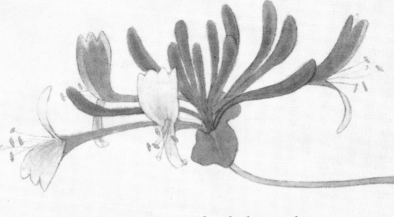

Bats can see. But in the dark, good ears are more useful than eyes.

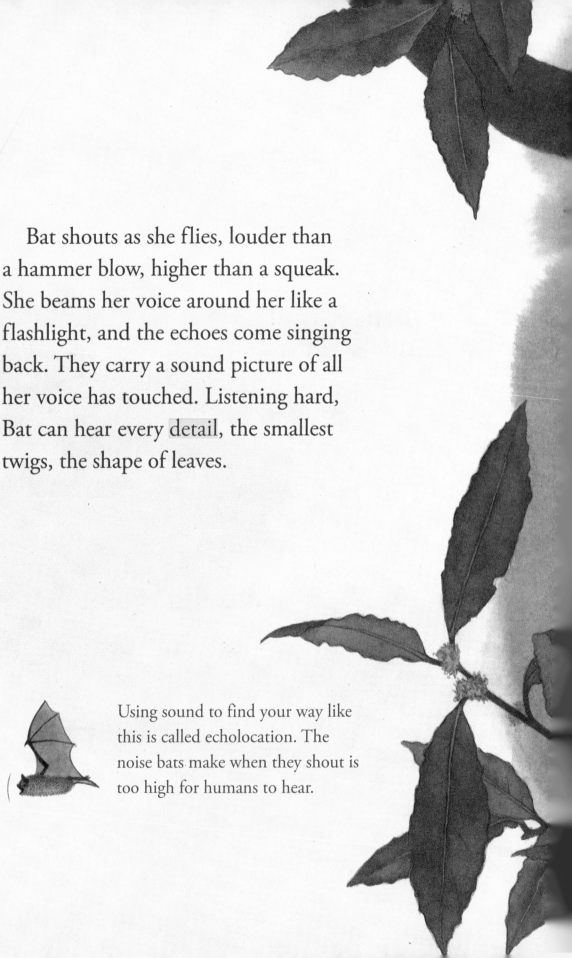

Bat shouts as she flies, louder than
a hammer blow, higher than a squeak.
She beams her voice around her like a
flashlight, and the echoes come singing
back. They carry a sound picture of all
her voice has touched. Listening hard,
Bat can hear every detail, the smallest
twigs, the shape of leaves.

Using sound to find your way like
this is called echolocation. The
noise bats make when they shout is
too high for humans to hear.

Gliding and fluttering
back and forth, she shouts
her torch of sound among the
trees, listening for her supper.

All is still. . . .

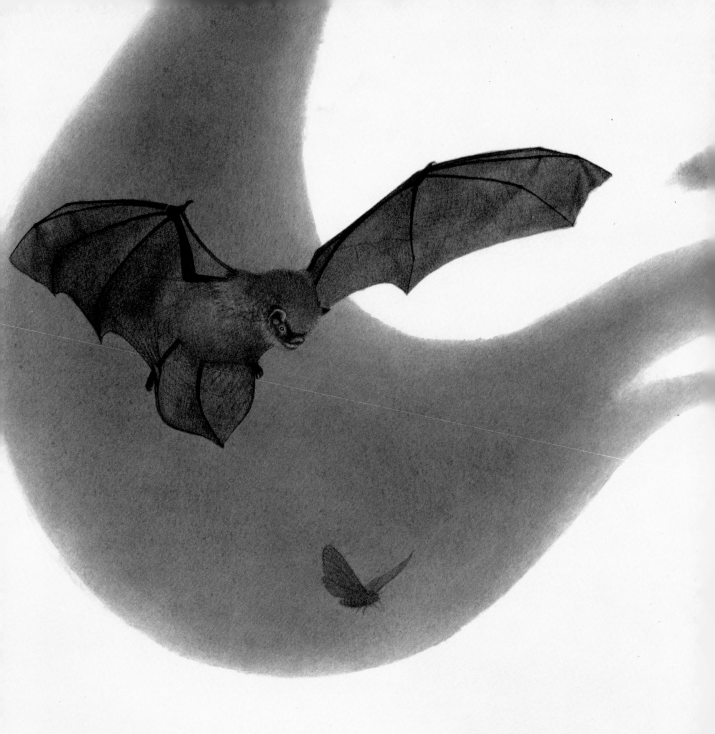

Then a fat moth takes flight below her.

Bat plunges, fast as blinking, and grabs it in her open mouth.

But the moth's pearly scales are moon-dust slippery. It slithers from between her teeth.

Bat dives, nets it with a wing tip, scoops it to her mouth.

This time she bites hard. Its wings fall
away, like the wrapper from a candy. In a
moment the moth is eaten. Bat sneezes.
The dusty scales got up her nose.

A bat can eat dozens
of big moths in a single
night—or thousands
of tiny flies, gnats, and
mosquitoes.

Most species of bats eat
insects, but there are some
that eat fruit, fish, frogs,
even blood!

Hunting time has run out. The dark will soon be gone. In the east, the sky is getting light. It's past Bat's bedtime.

She flies to the roof in the last shadows and swoops in under the broken tile.

The place where bats sleep in the day is called a roost. It can be in a building, a cave, or a tree, so long as it's dry and safe.

Baby bats can't fly. Sometimes mother bats carry their babies when they go out, but mostly the babies stay behind in the roost and crowd together to keep warm.

Inside, there are squeakings. Fifty hungry batlings hang in a huddle, hooked to a rafter by oversized feet. Bat lands and pushes in among them, toes first, upside down again.

Bat knows her baby's voice, and calls to it. The velvet scrap batling climbs aboard and clings to Bat's fur by its coat-hanger feet. Wrapped in her leathery wings, the baby snuggles to sleep.

Baby bats drink mother's milk until they learn to fly at a few weeks old. Then they can leave the roost at night to find their own food.

Bats are nocturnal. That means they rest by day and come out at night to search for food.

Outside, the birds are singing. The flowers turn their faces to the sun. But inside the roof hole, the darkness stays. Bat dozes with her batling, waiting.

When the tide of night rises again, Bat will wake and plunge into the blackness, shouting.

Bat loves the night.

THINK CRITICALLY

① What does a bat do each night? Tell the main events in order. SEQUENCE

② Do you think the author wrote this story to entertain, to inform, or both? Explain your answer. AUTHOR'S PURPOSE

③ Do you think your community should protect places where bats can live? Why or why not?

EXPRESS PERSONAL OPINIONS

④ Why do bats hunt for moths and insects at night? DRAW CONCLUSIONS

⑤ **WRITE** Why do baby bats need other bats to survive? Use details and examples from the selection to explain your answer. SHORT RESPONSE

Meet the Author

NICOLA DAVIES

Nicola Davies has always been interested in animals. As a child, she spent much of her time in the garden with her grandfather. There, among the flowers, she loved to look at ants and bird nests.

After college, Nicola Davies worked as a zoologist. She studied bats, geese, and whales. She also wanted to write about animals, but many years passed before she did. Now Nicola Davies combines her love of animals and her writing. She has written books about sharks, turtles, and polar bears.

Nicola Davies lives in Wales. At night, she loves to watch the bats that nest in the roof of her cottage.

 www.harcourtschool.com/storytown

Meet the Illustrator

SARAH FOX-DAVIES

Sarah Fox-Davies likes to draw animals in their natural environments. Her drawings of bats, beavers, bears, and other animals have appeared in many different magazines and children's books. She also illustrates nature and gardening books. Sarah Fox-Davies used pencils and watercolors to create the realistic illustrations for this book.

Fox-Davies lives in Wales. While she was making the illustrations for *Bat Loves the Night*, a bat flew into her studio. It landed right on her desk!

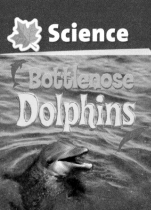

Magazine Article

Do you hear those sounds? They're the squeaking and squawking, clicking and whistling of deep-sea mammals that just love to talk. Meet the chatty . . .

Bottlenose Dolphins

from *Chickadee* magazine

Dolphins are big talkers! They spend lots of time yapping to each other under water in the ocean. Every dolphin is born with a special whistle, or clicking sound. A mother dolphin and her baby use the sounds to find each other if they separate. Dolphins call each other by name when they play by copying the sound of their friends' whistle.

Click → Echo

The sounds that dolphins make are not just for talking. They use clicking sounds to find their food. The sounds travel from the dolphin's head, then bounce off fish, or other things the dolphin eats. When the sounds return, the dolphin knows where the food is. This skill is called echolocation. (An echo is a sound that bounces off something so you hear it again. *Location* means "place.") What an awesome way to find a tasty treat!

Creature Features

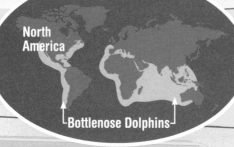

North America

Bottlenose Dolphins

Bottlenose dolphins live in warm oceans all over the world.

Dolphins sometimes jump up and "walk" on their tails on the water.

A dolphin is almost three times bigger than you!

Connections

Comparing Texts

1. How do bats and dolphins use echolocation differently? How do they use it in the same way?

2. Did you learn anything that changed your opinion about bats? Explain your answer.

3. In "Bat Loves the Night," what does the bat need to survive?

Vocabulary Review

The bat swoops down with little effort.

Word Pairs

Work with a partner. Write each Vocabulary Word on a card. Place the cards face down. Take turns flipping over two cards and writing a sentence that uses both words. Read your sentences to your partner and decide whether the Vocabulary Words are used correctly.

nocturnal

effort

dozes

swoops

detail

fluttering

Fluency Practice

Repeated Reading

Choose a section of "Bat Loves the Night." Use a stopwatch to time yourself as you read. Try to improve your reading time as you practice the section. Repeat the section until you can read it with no mistakes.

Writing

Write an Explanation

Write an explanation of how the bat in "Bat Loves the Night" hunts for food. Use the chart to help you organize the sequence of events.

My Writing Checklist

Writing Trait ▶ Sentence Fluency

✔ I tell events in the order they happen.

✔ My sentences connect to the main idea.

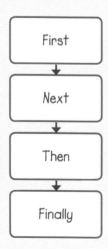

First

↓

Next

↓

Then

↓

Finally

Big 💡 Idea

Fantasy stories use unrealistic characters and story events.

Enduring ❗ Understanding

Readers use the clue words *because, so, if,* and *then* to understand the cause-and-effect relationships of the characters or events.

Essential ❓ Question

What word clues can readers use to determine cause-and-effect relationships?

Spelling Words

Words with Prefixes:
pre-, mis-, in-

input	preheat
preset	indoors
misuse	misplace
inside	preschool
preview	misread
incorrect	mismatch
pretest	misspell
mislead	

Challenge

mistaken	misprint
incomplete	invisible
misbehave	

Fluency

Expression

Comprehension

 Cause and Effect

 Answer Questions

Robust Vocabulary

eagerly

transferred

fondness

emotion

ridiculous

disgraceful

decent

inherit

contented

collaborate

Phonics

Words with Prefixes:
pre-, mis-, in-

Writing

• Fantasy
• Organization

Lesson 23

Genre: Fantasy

Chestnut Cove

WRITTEN AND ILLUSTRATED BY TIM EGAN

Mayors

by Shannon Knudsen

Genre: Expository Nonfiction

Phonics Skill

Prefixes *pre-*, *mis-*, *in-*

A **prefix** is a word part that is added to the beginning of a word. A prefix usually changes a word's meaning. Read these prefixes and their meanings.

Prefix	Meaning
pre-	before
mis-	badly or wrongly
in-	not

To read longer words, look for prefixes that you know. Here are some tips:

- Note that a prefix usually adds a syllable to the beginning of a word.

- Use the meaning of the prefix to help you figure out the meaning of the word.

Use what you know about prefixes to help you read and understand this story.

The queen asked the new cook, Larry, to make a pie for the king. First, Larry <u>preheated</u> the oven. The oven was <u>inexact</u>, so he turned it to the hottest setting.

Larry <u>misread</u> the amount of salt needed and poured in the whole container. He <u>misjudged</u> the size of the pan, and the pie filling spilled all over the oven. The pie burned to a crisp. The queen said, "You're the most <u>inexperienced</u> cook I've met!" She took back the money she had <u>prepaid</u> Larry.

Try This!

Look back at the story. Use what you know to read aloud each underlined word. Then tell what you think each word in the story means.

 www.harcourtschool.com/storytown

Vocabulary

fondness

emotion

ridiculous

disgraceful

decent

inherit

The Duck's New Home

Saturday, April 20

Today I went to the park to count ducklings. I have a **fondness** for ducks. I was filled with **emotion** because I found a lost duckling. The rest of the ducks had flown away. When I got home, I asked Mother if I could bring the duckling to live in our castle.

"Don't be **ridiculous**," she told me. "Ducks don't live in castles."

I felt sad.

Sunday, April 21

Today, I visited the duckling again. "It's **disgraceful** that the ducks left you," I said. "I will help you find a better home."

At dinner, I said to Mother, "Our castle pond is perfect for ducks. The duckling could live with the swans."

Mother finally agreed. "You are a **decent** girl," she said. "You will be a great queen when you **inherit** my throne."

That made me happy!

 www.harcourtschool.com/storytown

Word Champion

Your mission this week is to use Vocabulary Words in conversation. For example, tell a classmate about a time when something ridiculous happened. Write in your vocabulary journal the sentences in which you used Vocabulary Words.

Award-Winning Author

Chestnut Cove

WRITTEN AND ILLUSTRATED BY TIM EGAN

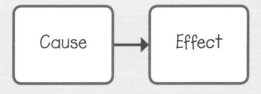

Fantasy

Genre Study

A **fantasy** is a story that could not happen in real life. Look for

- characters who may or may not be realistic.

- something that causes other events to happen.

Cause → Effect

Comprehension Strategy

As you read, look for information that helps you **answer questions** you might have.

228

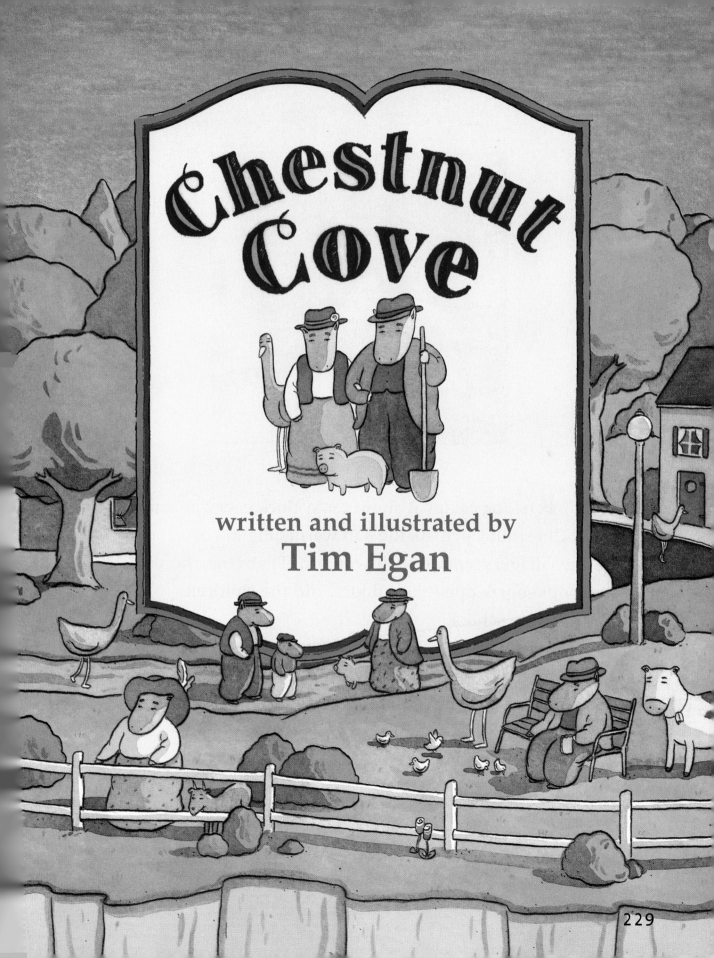

Chestnut Cove

written and illustrated by
Tim Egan

The fog clears at about ten o'clock every morning at Chestnut Cove. As the sun warms the town, the villagers tend to their wonderful gardens, the shopkeepers open their doors, and the children trot off to school.

You can usually find Mrs. Lark strolling along the cliffside with her pig, Eloise. And sometimes you might see the Ferguson family having somersault races in the town square.

Mrs. Ferguson wins most of the time.

Interesting things are always happening in Chestnut Cove. Like when Joe Morgan's cow, Thelma, got stuck way up in an oak tree. It took half the town to get her down.

Everyone's still trying to figure out how she got up there.

Another time, the Fergusons' fish drank up their pond. There was a frantic rush to get him to the lake as quickly as possible. As strange as things may get, everybody always tries to help one another out.

Well, one day late last winter, the town was
awakened by the sounds of bells and trumpets. It was
the ship of King Milford — a cause for excitement. It
was also seven o'clock in the morning, and though
some folks didn't seem quite ready to get up, they
did anyway.

King Milford was a fine leader, and most everyone
liked him. He wore a top hat instead of a crown and
had a rather strange fondness for watermelons, but
he was a fair and decent ruler.

The king lived in a magnificent castle on a nearby island. He had been traveling for three days to each and every village in the land with the same incredible announcement. "Whosoever grows the largest and juiciest watermelon by summer's end shall inherit my entire kingdom. Good luck!" he said.

Then he left.

Everyone laughed at the whole ridiculous idea and went on with the day as usual.

Some folks just went back to bed.

But over the next few days, the villagers started thinking about all the wonderful things they could have if they inherited the king's riches.

Mrs. Phillips imagined all the beautiful dresses and fancy hats she could buy. She just loved fancy hats.

And the Johnsons knew they could build a bigger ranch and have a lot more pets . . . as if they needed more pets.

Joe Morgan could buy the nicest wagon in the land. He was suddenly tired of his old wagon, even though he had built it himself.

And Mr. Ferguson could buy his own ship, which he and his family could sail away on. It was endless how much they didn't have.

The following week was quieter than usual. Everyone was busy gardening, turning the soil and planting watermelons.

As the weeks went by and the melons began to grow, the villagers of Chestnut Cove began to change. They didn't talk to each other as much because they were all so busy. Some of them even built fences around their gardens so that no one could touch their watermelons.

It seemed that Mrs. Lark was growing the largest one. It was bigger than Eloise the pig, yet smaller than Thelma the cow.

Mrs. Lark started sleeping in her garden at night so that nobody could steal her amazing watermelon.

Joe Morgan's watermelon was pretty impressive, too. He stood guard all day with Thelma. Things weren't good.

You could tell everything had changed when, one day, Mrs. Phillips's goat got his horns stuck in the park bench and nobody, not even Mrs. Phillips, was there to help.

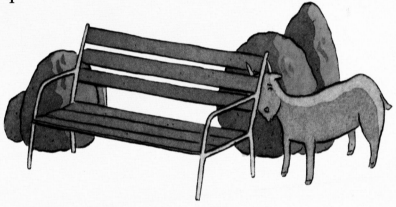

By harvest time, things were even worse. Everyone was fighting over who had the best watermelon. The king was coming the next day and they all worked late into the afternoon preparing. The streets were crowded but no one was saying a word.

Then, just as the sun was going down, Mrs. Lark came running into the town screaming, "It's Eloise! She's fallen off the cliff! My poor little pig is stuck on a ledge. Please, can't somebody help?"

Well, in a moment the whole town went running
toward the cliff. Everyone knew and loved Eloise, and
would do anything to save that little pig.

It was a tremendous effort. They brought rope and shovels and hammers and wrenches. Of course, all they needed was the rope, so they put the other stuff down and lowered Joe Morgan along the side of the cliff toward Eloise.

It was scary and great at the same time.

When it was over, about twenty minutes later, Eloise and Joe were safe. Mrs. Lark, her eyes filled with emotion, stood up and said, "Thank you all so much. And, um, nothing against Milford, the watermelon king, but I personally think this whole contest is, well . . . silly. In fact, I'm going to go home and eat mine before he even sees it. Would anyone care to join me?"

Everyone was quiet for a moment. Then one of the Ferguson kids yelled, "Picnic in the town square!"

Five minutes later, everybody gathered at the square with breads and cheeses and drinks and shovels. Once again, they didn't need the shovels, but someone kept bringing them anyway.

Oh, and they brought watermelons. The most beautiful watermelons that anyone had ever seen.

They danced and ate all night long. When it was over, the only watermelons that were left were a few rotten-looking ones.

The next morning, as expected, the king showed up. He looked at the watermelons that were left.

He wasn't very impressed.

As he boarded his ship he said, "I'm afraid these are the most disappointing watermelons I've seen yet. They are, quite frankly, disgraceful. I believe you all need to work on your gardening skills."

And as his ship pulled away, the villagers of Chestnut Cove looked rather sad.

But they weren't sad at all, they were just tired from staying up all night.

Think Critically

1. Why do the villagers want to grow the largest and juiciest watermelons?  CAUSE/EFFECT

2. How does the watermelon-growing contest change the villagers? MAKE INFERENCES

3. What does the author think about the way the villagers change during the contest? How do you know? AUTHOR'S VIEWPOINT

4. Why aren't the villagers sad about losing the contest? DRAW CONCLUSIONS

5. WRITE Describe how the activities of the community change throughout the story. Use details from the story to explain your answer.
   EXTENDED RESPONSE

Tim Egan

Tim Egan didn't always write and illustrate children's books. He had another job, but his wife noticed that he was always drawing pictures of pigs, ducks, and other characters. One day she told him that he should try to make a children's book. He has been making children's books ever since.

Tim Egan's first stories were long and serious. Then he started writing funnier ones. These books were more fun to work on, so he worked even harder to make them right. Most of the time, Tim Egan starts a book by drawing characters. Then he starts writing about the characters. He finds that if he likes the characters, other people will usually like them too.

GO online www.harcourtschool.com/storytown

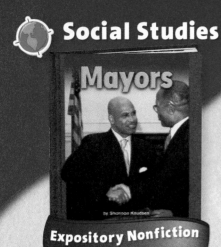

Expository Nonfiction

MAYORS

by Shannon Knudsen

Who is the leader of your community? Many communities have a leader called a mayor. Mayors work to make their communities better places to live. Mayors in different cities and towns do different jobs.

What are some jobs that mayors do?

Some mayors run groups of workers called departments. Each department helps the community in different ways. The police department fights crime. The fire department fights fires.

Mayors work to make schools better. Mayors talk to principals, teachers, and kids about how to help kids learn.

Mayors also help make laws. They meet with a group called the city council. The council talks about new laws. It decides how to spend the community's money.

Mayors help make a community a nice place to live. When important visitors come to a city, the mayor may show them around town.

Mayors honor people who have helped the community. They give awards for jobs well done. Mayors help people celebrate, too. A mayor might attend a special school event.

How does someone become a mayor?

In most places, the mayor is chosen by the adults who live there. The people who run for mayor are called candidates. Candidates make speeches. They tell people their ideas about how to run the community. Candidates also meet people and talk with them. Sometimes they meet to talk about how their ideas are different.

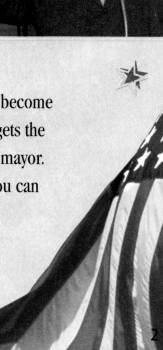

It is election day! Adults vote for the person they want to become the mayor. Then the votes are counted. The candidate who gets the most votes wins the election. That person becomes the new mayor.

Mayors lead our communities in many ways. Someday you can help choose your mayor by voting. Maybe you will run for mayor yourself!

Connections

Comparing Texts

1. Think about the king in "Chestnut Cove." How is he like a mayor?

2. What contest do you know about? Describe the contest.

3. How are the villagers in the story like people in a real community? How are they different?

Vocabulary Review

Word Webs

Work with a partner. Create word webs for two Vocabulary Words. Put the Vocabulary Word in the center of your web. Then write related words in the web. Explain how each word in your web is related to the Vocabulary Word.

fondness

emotion

ridiculous

disgraceful

decent

inherit

enjoy — fondness

like

Fluency Practice

Readers' Theater

Work with a small group. Choose characters and read a page from "Chestnut Cove" as Readers' Theater. Read with expression to show the characters' feelings. Ask listeners to tell what they liked about the reading.

Writing

Write a Cause-and-Effect Paragraph

Think about what happens in "Chestnut Cove" when Eloise falls off the cliff. Write a paragraph to describe a cause and its effects. Use a cause–effect chart to organize your notes before you begin to write.

My Writing Checklist

Writing Trait ▶ Organization

✔ I use a cause-effect chart to plan my story.

✔ I use words such as *first*, *next*, *then*, and *finally* to show time order.

Cause	→	Effect

Big Idea
Realistic fiction presents fictional text as if it really occurred.

Enduring ! Understanding
Readers use the clue words *so, because, to,* and *since* to understand cause-and-effect relationships.

Essential ? Question
How do readers determine the cause-and-effect relationships in realistic fiction?

Spelling Words

Words with Schwa /ə/

upon	across
above	agree
cover	ever
apart	amount
either	ahead
alike	alive
awake	around
afraid	

Challenge

among	applause
again	appear
about	

Fluency

Expression

Robust Vocabulary

- affordable
- individually
- clutter
- visible
- mentioned
- beckoned
- flustered
- remark
- presentation
- effective

Comprehension

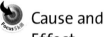 Cause and Effect

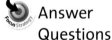 Answer Questions

Phonics

Words with Schwa /ə/

Writing

- Persuasion
- Organization

Genre: Realistic Fiction

BEVERLY CLEARY
RAMONA QUIMBY, AGE 8

Being a member of the
Quimby family in
the third grade
is harder than
Ram
e

SLAM DUNK
WATER

Genre: Advertisement

255

Cause and Effect

In stories, one event is often the reason that another event happens. The reason something happens is the **cause.** What happens is the **effect.** Authors often use signal words like these to show causes and effects.

because	*so that*	*since*	*as a result*
therefore	*in order to*	*so*	*for this reason*

Identifying causes and effects helps you understand why events happen in a story.

Cause	→	Effect

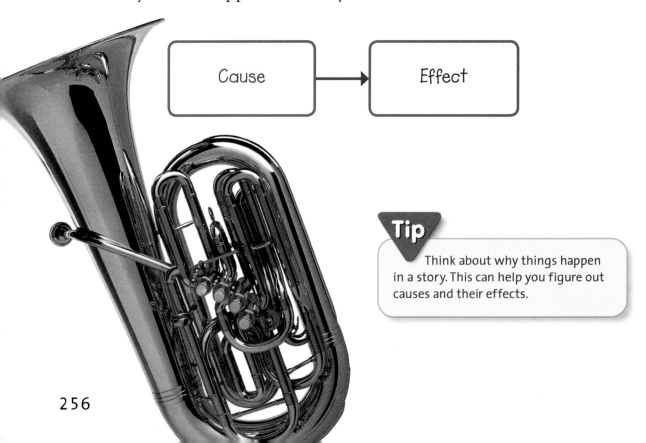

Tip

Think about why things happen in a story. This can help you figure out causes and their effects.

Read the story below. Then use the chart to tell about a cause and its effect.

Fred loved to play his tuba. He liked its low, rich sound. He played it morning, noon, and night. His dog often howled along with him.

Fred went to a tryout to join his school's band. He did not get in because he played too loudly.

At home he asked his mother, "What can I do?" Fred's mother played the piano while he played. He listened to the piano and soon he could play the song with his mother. "Now I know to play softly when I play along with others," Fred said.

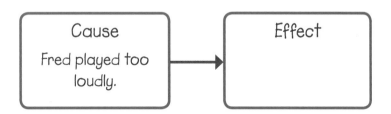

Cause		Effect
Fred played too loudly.	→	

Try This!

Look back at this passage. What happened because Fred listened as his mother played the piano?

www.harcourtschool.com/storytown

Vocabulary

clutter

visible

mentioned

beckoned

remark

flustered

Mark's Journal

Monday, January 12

My room is full of **clutter**. I have so many collections that my floor is barely **visible**. I collect stamps, rocks, pennies, trading cards, and many other things.

I had **mentioned** to my father that I needed more space to store things. Today he stood in my bedroom doorway and **beckoned** to me. He showed me the shelves he had bought just for me!

Tuesday, January 13

After I put all of my things on my new shelves, I showed the room to my father. He made a wise **remark**. He said, "Your new shelves look great. Now you won't feel **flustered** when you need to find something. Everything in your room has a place where it belongs."

 www.harcourtschool.com/storytown

Word Scribe

 Your task this week is to use the Vocabulary Words in your writing. For example, you could write about a time that you felt flustered. Share your writing with your classmates.

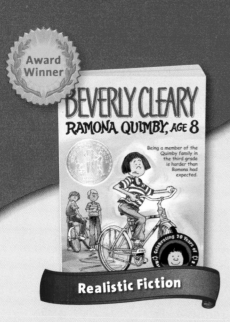

Realistic Fiction

Genre Study

Realistic fiction stories have characters and settings that could be real. Look for

- characters with realistic problems.

- cause-and-effect relationships like those in real life.

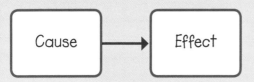

| Cause | → | Effect |

Comprehension Strategy

Answer questions that you have or that your teacher asks to better understand what you read.

na Quimby, Age 8

by
Beverly Cleary

illustrated by
Anne-Sophie Lanquetin

Two days ago, Ramona became sick at school and had to leave early. Now she is at home, worrying about what her classmates will think of her. She thinks that Danny might make fun of her for being sick. Ramona secretly refers to Danny as "Yard Ape" because he always seems to be noisily running around the schoolyard.

To pass the time at home, Ramona has been watching TV commercials. After a talk with her father, Ramona realizes that the purpose of commercials is to sell something.

In the meantime, Ramona's teacher, Mrs. Whaley, has sent a homework assignment. Ramona has to write a book report about a book called The Left-Behind Cat. Mrs. Whaley wants the students to pretend they are selling the book to someone. Ramona's sister, Beezus, says that most book reports sound alike, so Ramona is eager to make hers exciting.

Ramona's Book Report

Ramona went to her room and looked at her table, which the family called "Ramona's studio," because it was a clutter of crayons, different kinds of paper, tape, bits of yarn, and odds and ends that Ramona used for amusing herself. Then Ramona thought a moment, and suddenly, filled with inspiration, she went to work. She knew exactly what she wanted to do and set about doing it. She worked with paper, crayons, tape, and rubber bands. She worked so hard and with such pleasure that her cheeks grew pink. Nothing in the whole world felt as good as being able to make something from a sudden idea.

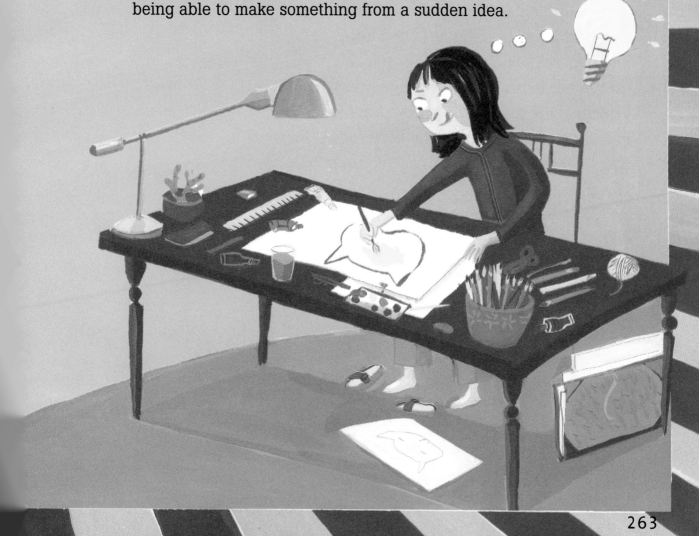

Finally, with a big sigh of relief, Ramona leaned back in her chair to admire her work: three cat masks with holes for eyes and mouths, masks that could be worn by hooking rubber bands over ears. But Ramona did not stop there. With pencil and paper, she began to write out what she would say. She was so full of ideas that she printed rather than waste time in cursive writing. Next she phoned Sara and Janet, keeping her voice low and trying not to giggle so she wouldn't disturb her father any more than necessary, and explained her plan to them. Both her friends giggled and agreed to take part in the book report. Ramona spent the rest of the evening memorizing what she was going to say.

The next morning on the bus and at school, no one even mentioned Ramona's throwing up. She had braced herself for some remark from Yard Ape, but all he said was "Hi, Superfoot."

When school started, Ramona slipped cat masks to Sara and Janet, handed her written excuse for her absence to Mrs. Whaley, and waited, fanning away escaped fruit flies, for book reports to begin.

After arithmetic, Mrs. Whaley called on several people to come to the front of the room to pretend they were selling books to the class. Most of the reports began, "This is a book about . . ." and many, as Beezus had predicted, ended with ". . . if you want to find out what happens next, read the book."

Then Mrs. Whaley said, "We have time for one more report before lunch. Who wants to be next?"

Ramona waved her hand, and Mrs. Whaley nodded.

Ramona beckoned to Sara and Janet, who giggled in an embarrassed way but joined Ramona, standing behind her and off to one side. All three girls slipped on their cat masks and giggled again. Ramona took a deep breath as Sara and Janet began to chant, "*Meow*, meow, meow, meow. *Meow*, meow, meow, meow," and danced back and forth like the cats they had seen in the cat-food commercial on television.

"*Left-Behind Cat* gives kids something to smile about," said Ramona in a loud clear voice, while her chorus meowed softly behind her. She wasn't sure that what she said was exactly true, but neither were the commercials that showed cats eating dry cat food without making any noise. "Kids who have tried *Left-Behind Cat* are all smiles, smiles, smiles. *Left-Behind Cat* is the book kids ask for by name. Kids can read it every day and thrive on it. The happiest kids read *Left-Behind Cat*. *Left-Behind Cat* contains cats, dogs, people—" Here Ramona caught sight of Yard Ape leaning back in his seat, grinning in the way that always flustered her. She could not help interrupting herself with a giggle,

and after suppressing it she tried not to look at Yard Ape and to take up where she had left off. ". . . cats, dogs, people—" The giggle came back, and Ramona was lost. She could not remember what came next. " . . . cats, dogs, people," she repeated, trying to start and failing.

Mrs. Whaley and the class waited. Yard Ape grinned. Ramona's loyal chorus meowed and danced. This performance could not go on all morning. Ramona had to say something, anything to end the waiting, the meowing, her book report. She tried desperately to recall a cat-food commercial, any cat-food commercial, and could not. All she could remember was the man on television who ate the pizza, and so she blurted out the only sentence she could think of, "I can't believe I read the *whole* thing!"

Mrs. Whaley's laugh rang out above the laughter of the class. Ramona felt her face turn red behind her mask, and her ears, visible to the class, turned red as well.

"Thank you Ramona," said Mrs. Whaley. "That was most entertaining. Class, you are excused for lunch."

Ramona felt brave behind her cat mask. "Mrs. Whaley," she said as the class pushed back chairs and gathered up lunch boxes, "that wasn't the way my report was supposed to end."

"Did you like the book?" asked Mrs. Whaley.

"Not really," confessed Ramona.

"Then I think it was a good way to end your report," said the teacher.

Think Critically

1. What happens because Yard Ape grins at Ramona during her book report? CAUSE/EFFECT

2. How does the author let readers know that Ramona is creative? DRAW CONCLUSIONS

3. What would you do if you had to pretend to "sell" a book you didn't like? EXPRESS PERSONAL OPINIONS

4. How does Ramona solve her problem at the end of the book report? PROBLEM/SOLUTION

5. **WRITE** Write about a time you did something funny or creative. SHORT RESPONSE

Meet the Author
Beverly Cleary

Beverly Cleary once lived in a town so small that it didn't even have a library. When she moved to Portland, Oregon, Beverly Cleary spent a lot of time at the library.

Beverly Cleary became a librarian. Some of the children she met asked, "Where are the books about kids like us?" The answer came in Beverly Cleary's first book, *Henry Huggins*. In that book was a girl named Ramona Quimby.

Today there's a statue of Ramona Quimby in the neighborhood park where Beverly Cleary once lived. It is the same neighborhood where the books featuring Ramona take place.

 GO online www.harcourtschool.com/storytown

SLAM DUNK
WATER

Advertisements are used to sell products and services. Suppose Slam Dunk Water is a new drink for people who play sports. Read these examples to learn about some different kinds of advertisements.

You might see this kind of advertisement on the side of the road. It is called a billboard ad.

This is a fact. It can be proved.

YOUR BODY NEEDS WATER TO STAY HEALTHY!

THE BEST WATER OUT THERE IS
SLAM DUNK
WATER

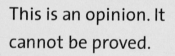

This is an opinion. It cannot be proved.

An ad in a magazine might look like this.

When I play for the Goodsville Tigers, I always drink SLAM DUNK WATER. SLAM DUNK WATER keeps me going!

Some advertisements show famous people supporting a product or service. This is called an **endorsement**.

SLAM DUNK
WATER

Every play is a slam dunk when you drink SLAM DUNK WATER

Advertisements often have a slogan or catchy phrase.

Connections

Comparing Texts

1. How is Ramona's book report like an advertisement? How is it different?

2. What part of the story did you think was funny? Why?

3. How is Ramona's school like your school? Give details.

Vocabulary Review

Vocabulary Sort

Work with a partner. Make a chart with two columns: "Words about a Setting" and "What a Character Does." Write each Vocabulary Word in one of the categories. Then talk about why the word belongs in that category.

clutter

visible

mentioned

beckoned

flustered

remark

Fluency Practice

Partner Reading

Work with a partner. Take turns reading a page from "Ramona's Book Report." Focus on reading with expression. Use your voice to show how the characters are feeling. Have your partner tell you what he or she liked about the reading.

Writing

Write an Ad

Write an advertisement for a favorite product. Explain why someone should use this product. Use a cause-effect chart to help you plan your writing.

My Writing Checklist

Writing Trait ▸ Organization

✔ I use a cause-effect chart to plan my writing.

✔ My organization makes sense.

Cause → Effect

Big Idea
Science fiction includes cause-and-effect relationships in time-order events.

Enduring ! Understanding
Readers use time-order events to understand the cause-and-effect relationships.

Essential ? Question
Why do readers use the cause-and-effect relationships and time-order events to understand science fiction?

Spelling Words

Review

choose	threw
false	apart
booth	soft
preschool	across
foot	cause
misspell	around
bruise	thaw
indoors	

Fluency

Review Reading Rate, Expression

Comprehension

Review
 Sequence, Cause and Effect

 Monitor Comprehension: Reread, Answer Questions

Robust Vocabulary

- required
- functional
- inhabitants
- amazement
- ample
- responsibility
- futuristic
- realistic
- confused
- shifting

Phonics

Review
- Words with /o͞o/oo, ew, ue, ui; /o͝o/oo
- Words with /ô/o, au(gh), aw, a(l), ough;
- Words with Prefixes: *pre-, mis-, in-*
- Words with Schwa /ə/

Writing

- *Review* Sentence Fluency, Organization
- Revise and Publish

Readers' Theater
SCIENCE FICTION

The **ROBODOGS**
of Greenville

illustrated by John Hovell

Content-Area Reading
SOCIAL STUDIES TEXTBOOK

YOUR
Social Studies
TEXTBOOK

required

functional

inhabitants

amazement

ample

responsibility

Reading for Fluency

When you read a script aloud,

- read at the same speed at which you would speak to a friend.

- use your voice to express the way your character is feeling.

The ROBODOGS of Greenville

illustrated by John Hovell

Characters

Narrator	Robodog
Diz	Professor
Cosmo	Captain Spacely

Setting: A town on Earth in the future

Narrator: This story takes place in the year 2222 in a small town called Greenville. Greenville is a friendly little community, just like many other towns. Everyone gets along there.

Diz: Hi, Cosmo! Thanks for coming over.

Cosmo: Anytime, Diz! How are things over at your dad's hydro car store?

Diz: Really busy, Cosmo.

Cosmo: I hear they're selling those hydro cars faster than the factory on planet Mars can make them!

Narrator: Diz and Cosmo live with their families in Greenville. Their parents fly the children to school in the family hydro cars. The children chat with their friends each evening on the family televideocomputers. They also play with their family dogs.

Diz: Here, Robodog! Catch the flying disk!

Robodog: I am coming, Owner Diz. I will catch the disk.

Narrator: There is one unusual thing about the dogs in Greenville. All the dogs are robots.

Diz: Good catch, Robodog.

Robodog: Thank you, Owner Diz. What can I do for you now?

Narrator: The robodog is the only kind of dog in Greenville. Scientists have built robodogs to be better than real dogs. They can speak. They can take care of chores that would have required effort, such as cleaning and cooking. They can even beam movies from their eyes onto a wall!

Fluency Tip

Think about what a robot dog might sound like if it spoke.

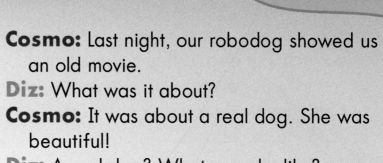

Cosmo: Last night, our robodog showed us an old movie.

Diz: What was it about?

Cosmo: It was about a real dog. She was beautiful!

Diz: A real dog? What was she like?

Cosmo: A lot like our robodogs. She could do tricks and help her owners.

Diz: Could she speak?

Cosmo: She could only make a sound called barking. She didn't know any human words.

Diz: Really? That's strange.

Robodog: Yes. That is very strange, Owner Diz.

Cosmo: Robodog, I'm hungry. Would you go to the kitchen and make sandwiches for Diz and me, please?

Robodog: Should I do that, Owner Diz?

Diz: It's okay, Robodog. Cosmo's robodog is at home. You can follow Cosmo's commands, too.

Robodog: I will be right back, Owner Diz and Friend Cosmo.

Cosmo: The dog in the movie seemed to love her owner. She was sweet and cuddly. She didn't just work around the house.

Diz: The dog loved her owner? That sounds strange.

Cosmo: It was nice, really. The dog and her owner were best friends.

Diz: I wish my robodog were like that.

Narrator: You see, robodogs are helpful and can do tricks, but they are not sweet or cuddly.

Cosmo: Maybe we should talk to the professor about this.

Narrator: The professor is an expert on animals. So Diz and Cosmo go to talk to the professor about the differences between real dogs and robodogs.

Professor: Yes, Diz and Cosmo. It is true that real dogs had emotions, while robodogs do not. Real dogs could be happy or sad. They could even show love.

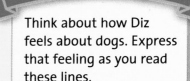

Fluency Tip

Think about how Diz feels about dogs. Express that feeling as you read these lines.

Dog — Happy — Sad

Robodog — No Emotions

Diz: Why don't our robodogs show emotion?

Professor: Scientists do not know how to make dogs that act like friends. They can make them useful but not loving.

Cosmo: My robodog is very functional. It cleans my room, makes my meals, and helps me with my homework.

Diz: Robodogs aren't very cuddly!

Cosmo: I know. After Robodog has done its chores or tricks, it just switches off.

Professor: That's right. It dozes. The scientists made robodogs that way to save energy.

Diz: I wish I had a real dog.

Cosmo: There aren't any more real dogs. They disappeared permanently from Earth a hundred years ago.

Professor: It's funny that you should say that. I just got off my Intergalactic Computer Phone with the famous explorer Captain Spacely. He told me about an astonishing discovery. Maybe he can tell you about it, too. Computer Phone, call Captain Spacely.

Spacely: Captain Spacely here. Professor, do you want to hear more about my discovery?

Professor: Yes, indeed I do, Captain. Tell my friends Diz and Cosmo what you have found.

Spacely: I can do better than that. I'll show them what I've found!

Narrator: Captain Spacely steps away from the computer phone. Diz and Cosmo hear a whining sound. Then they hear barking.

Diz: What is that strange sound?

Cosmo: I heard that sound in the movie. It's the barking sound a real dog makes!

Narrator: Captain Spacely is visible on the screen again. Spacely beckons to a furry thing that leaps into his arms. Cosmo and Diz see that it looks like a robodog, but it acts differently.

Spacely: I've found real dogs! There is a small planet that has many of the same animals that were once on Earth. In fact, it has so many kinds of inhabitants that food and space are becoming scarce.

Narrator: The dog in Captain Spacely's arms wags its tail and licks his face. Diz and Cosmo look at the dog with amazement.

Diz: I wish I could have one of those dogs!

Cosmo: Me, too!

Fluency Tip

Captain Spacely is telling important details. Speak at a slower speed so that listeners can follow the story clearly.

Professor: I think that can be arranged. Tell them your plan, Captain Spacely!

Spacely: To help the animals, I am bringing a spaceship full of dogs back to Earth! There is ample room on Earth for dogs. Also, I know that people on Earth would take great care of them. Cosmo and Diz, caring for a dog takes a lot of responsibility. If you promise to care for them, you can have the first two!

Diz and **Cosmo:** Thanks, Captain Spacely!

Narrator: Sure enough, Captain Spacely brings real dogs back to Earth. Cosmo and Diz get the first two dogs.

Diz: Give me a hug, Scooter!

Cosmo: Here, Rascal! Come and play with me!

Narrator: As for the robodogs, Cosmo and Diz decide to keep them. They come in handy when it is time to give Scooter and Rascal a bath.

Robodog: Owner Cosmo, should I get Rascal's bath ready?

Cosmo: Yes, Robodog. After that, would you take Rascal out for a walk?

COMPREHENSION STRATEGIES
Review

Reading a Social Studies Textbook

Bridge to Content-Area Reading Social studies textbooks have special features that help you understand the text. These features include titles and headings, special vocabulary, and visual aids. Scan the pages for this information each time you read.

Read the notes on page 289. How can the features help you read a social studies lesson?

Review the Focus Strategies

You can also use the strategies you learned in this theme to help you read your social studies textbook.

Reread
Monitor your comprehension each time you read. If something you are reading doesn't make sense the first time, try rereading it.

Answer Questions
Use information you have read to answer questions at the end of sections. Look back in the text to check your answers.

As you read "Fighting for Our Freedoms" on pages 290–291, think about where and how to use the comprehension strategies.

TITLES AND HEADINGS
- The **lesson title** tells what the whole lesson will be about. The **headings** tell what each section will be about.

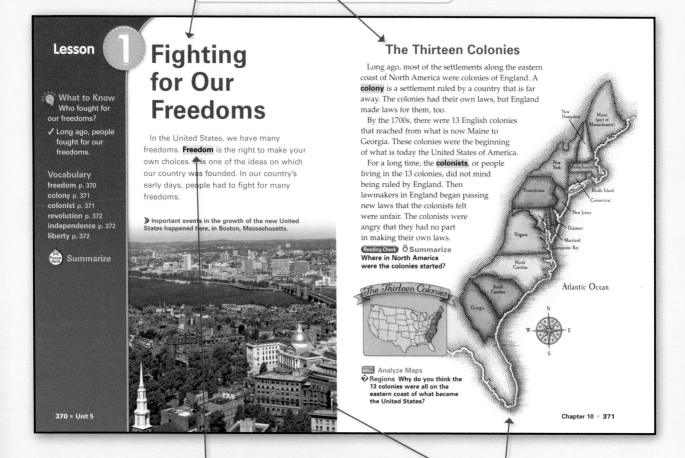

Lesson 1

Fighting for Our Freedoms

What to Know
Who fought for our freedoms?

✔ Long ago, people fought for our freedoms.

Vocabulary
freedom p. 370
colony p. 371
colonist p. 371
revolution p. 372
independence p. 372
liberty p. 372

Summarize

In the United States, we have many freedoms. **Freedom** is the right to make your own choices. It is one of the ideas on which our country was founded. In our country's early days, people had to fight for many freedoms.

▶ Important events in the growth of the new United States happened here, in Boston, Massachusetts.

The Thirteen Colonies

Long ago, most of the settlements along the eastern coast of North America were colonies of England. A **colony** is a settlement ruled by a country that is far away. The colonies had their own laws, but England made laws for them, too.

By the 1700s, there were 13 English colonies that reached from what is now Maine to Georgia. These colonies were the beginning of what is today the United States of America.

For a long time, the **colonists**, or people living in the 13 colonies, did not mind being ruled by England. Then lawmakers in England began passing new laws that the colonists felt were unfair. The colonists were angry that they had no part in making their own laws.

Reading Check **Summarize**
Where in North America were the colonies started?

The Thirteen Colonies

New Hampshire, Maine (part of Massachusetts), New York, Massachusetts, Rhode Island, Connecticut, Pennsylvania, New Jersey, Delaware, Maryland, Virginia, Chesapeake Bay, North Carolina, South Carolina, Georgia, Atlantic Ocean

Analyze Maps
➤ Regions Why do you think the 13 colonies were all on the eastern coast of what became the United States?

370 ▪ Unit 5

Chapter 10 ▪ 371

SPECIAL VOCABULARY
Social studies **vocabulary** words are usually boldfaced. The meaning of each word is given in the sentence.

VISUAL AIDS
Photographs with captions and **maps** give information at a glance. Maps help you locate places. Use the compass rose to tell north, south, east, and west.

289

Apply the Strategies Read these pages from a social studies textbook. As you read, stop and think about how you are using comprehension strategies.

Lesson 1

Fighting for Our Freedoms

What to Know
Who fought for our freedoms?

✓ Long ago, people fought for our freedoms.

Vocabulary
freedom p. 370
colony p. 371
colonist p. 371
revolution p. 372
independence p. 372
liberty p. 372

 Summarize

In the United States, we have many freedoms. **Freedom** is the right to make your own choices. It is one of the ideas on which our country was founded. In our country's early days, people had to fight for many freedoms.

❯ Important events in the growth of the new United States happened here, in Boston, Massachusetts.

Stop and Think

How could **rereading** help you **answer the questions** at the bottom of the page?

The Thirteen Colonies

Long ago, most of the settlements along the eastern coast of North America were colonies of England. A **colony** is a settlement ruled by a country that is far away. The colonies had their own laws, but England made laws for them, too.

By the 1700s, there were 13 English colonies that reached from what is now Maine to Georgia. These colonies were the beginning of what is today the United States of America.

For a long time, the **colonists**, or people living in the 13 colonies, did not mind being ruled by England. Then lawmakers in England began passing new laws that the colonists felt were unfair. The colonists were angry that they had no part in making their own laws.

Reading Check ŏ**Summarize**
Where in North America were the colonies started?

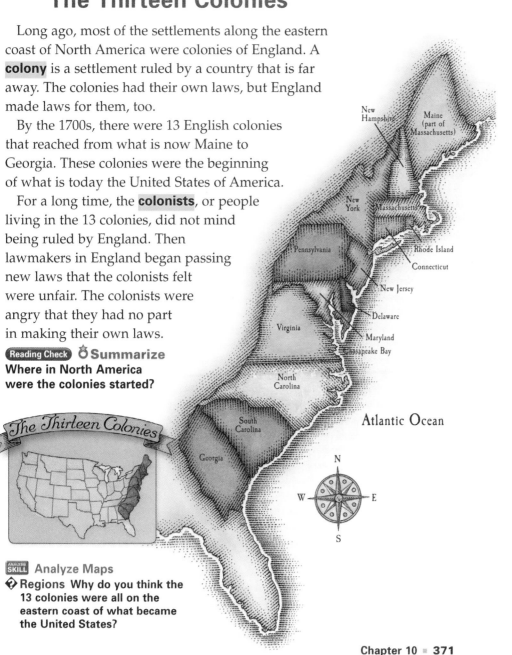

The Thirteen Colonies

Atlantic Ocean

Analyze Maps

SKILL

◆ **Regions** Why do you think the 13 colonies were all on the eastern coast of what became the United States?

Chapter 10 ▪ **371**

Theme 6 Discoveries

Starry Night, Vincent van Gogh

293

Big Idea
A fantasy story includes elements that are not realistic.

Enduring Understanding
Readers use hints or clues that make it possible to "read between the lines" to make inferences about a story.

Essential Question
How do readers use the clues that give deeper understanding to make inferences?

Spelling Words

Words with Suffixes -tion, -sion

section	question
caution	mention
fiction	station
nation	attention
action	portion
vision	collection
vacation	session
motion	

Challenge

admission	definition
discussion	description
decision	

Fluency
Punctuation

Comprehension
 Make Inferences

 Ask Questions

Robust Vocabulary
- bristly
- dreadful
- summoning
- nuisance
- sedentary
- oblige
- boasting
- sway
- adamant
- inevitable

Phonics
Words with Suffixes -tion, -sion

Writing
- Directions
- Word Choice

Lesson 26

Genre: Fantasy

Charlotte's Web

WINNER OF THE NEWBERY HONOR MEDAL

by E. B. WHITE
Author of STUART LITTLE
Pictures by GARTH WILLIAMS

CATERPILLARS SPIN WEBS, TOO!

by Shane F. McEvey

Genre: Expository Nonfiction

Make Inferences

Authors do not tell readers every detail about a story.
Readers need to figure out some things for themselves.
When readers add what they already know to what an
author has told them, they **make inferences.**

What the Author Tells Me	What I Already Know

Inference

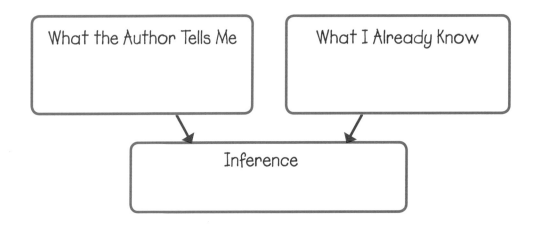

Tip

Use what you know from real
life to understand how a character
feels, what a character is like, and why
something happens.

Read the story. Then use the chart to make an inference.

> Margo, a trap-door spider, dug a hole in the earth and spun silk to make her burrow comfortable. The next morning, she watched her neighbor creep out of his burrow. His door was covered with gravel. "What are you doing?" she asked him.
>
> "Shh, I'm looking for my breakfast," the spider said.
>
> "Your door is hard to see," Margo said.
>
> "That's the point," he said. "I want to surprise passing insects to catch them."

What the Author Tells Me	What I Already Know
Margo's neighbor is looking for breakfast.	Spiders eat insects.

Inference

Try This!

Look back at this passage. What inference can you make about what Margo's neighbor is like?

 www.harcourtschool.com/storytown

Vocabulary

Build Robust Vocabulary

- summoning
- nuisance
- sedentary
- oblige
- boasting
- sway

Life on the Farm

Have you ever heard the sound of a rooster **summoning** a farmer to start the day? Farmers always have a lot of work to do, so they don't think the rooster's call is a **nuisance**. They don't have time to be **sedentary**. There is too much work to do!

The kind of work that farmers do depends on the kind of farm they have. Some farmers raise crops. Others raise animals.

The cow is ready to be milked. The farmer is glad to **oblige**.

Farmers who raise crops may grow grains, vegetables, or fruits. They make sure the plants get water to help them grow. After a good harvest, there is little time for **boasting**. It's time to plan the next year's crop.

Other farmers raise cows, pigs, or chickens. They feed and care for the animals. They keep barns and shelters clean so their animals will be safe and healthy.

When a wheat crop grows tall and healthy, it will **sway** in the breeze.

Go online www.harcourtschool.com/storytown

Word Detective

Your mission this week is to look for the Vocabulary Words in nonfiction books or magazine articles about farms and farm animals. Each time you read a Vocabulary Word, write it in your vocabulary journal. Tell where you found the word.

Fantasy

Genre Study

A **fantasy** is a story about events that could not really happen. Look for

- characters such as animals that do things real animals cannot do.

- a plot with a beginning, middle, and end.

```
Characters        Setting
          \      /
           Plot
```

Comprehension Strategy

Ask questions as you read. This will help you focus on the important ideas in a selection.

Charlotte's Web

by E. B. White   illustrated by Garth Williams

The barn on the Zuckermans' farm is a lively place. Fern, a girl who lives nearby, loves to visit the barn and watch the adventures of the animals. She has a special fondness for Wilbur, a pig that she helped to raise. Wilbur has lots of friends in the barn, including Charlotte the spider. Templeton the rat can be a nuisance, but he is Wilbur's friend, too. Several lambs and a family of geese add excitement to the barnyard where the animals spend their days.

Wilbur is still a young pig, and he has a lot to learn about the world around him. Luckily, Charlotte is a wise and patient friend.

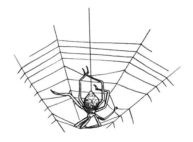

Wilbur's Boast

A spider's web is stronger than it looks. Although it is made of thin, delicate strands, the web is not easily broken. However, a web gets torn every day by the insects that kick around in it, and a spider must rebuild it when it gets full of holes. Charlotte liked to do her weaving during the late afternoon, and Fern liked to sit nearby and watch. One afternoon she heard a most interesting conversation and witnessed a strange event.

"You have awfully hairy legs, Charlotte," said Wilbur, as the spider busily worked at her task.

"My legs are hairy for a good reason," replied Charlotte. "Furthermore, each leg of mine has seven sections — the coxa, the trochanter, the femur, the patella, the tibia, the metatarsus, and the tarsus."

Wilbur sat bolt upright. "You're kidding," he said.

"No, I'm not, either."

"Say those names again, I didn't catch them the first time."

"Coxa, trochanter, femur, patella, tibia, metatarsus, and tarsus."

"Goodness!" said Wilbur, looking down at his own chubby legs. "I don't think *my* legs have seven sections."

"Well," said Charlotte, "you and I lead different lives. You don't have to spin a web. That takes real leg work."

"I could spin a web if I tried," said Wilbur, boasting. "I've just never tried."

"Let's see you do it," said Charlotte. Fern chuckled softly, and her eyes grew wide with love for the pig.

"O.K.," replied Wilbur. "You coach me and I'll spin one. It must be a lot of fun to spin a web. How do I start?"

"Take a deep breath!" said Charlotte, smiling. Wilbur breathed deeply. "Now climb to the highest place you can get to, like this." Charlotte raced up to the top of the doorway. Wilbur scrambled to the top of the manure pile.

"Very good!" said Charlotte. "Now make an attachment with your spinnerets, hurl yourself into space, and let out a dragline as you go down!"

Wilbur hesitated a moment, then jumped out into the air. He glanced hastily behind to see if a piece of rope was following him to check his fall, but nothing seemed to be happening in his rear, and the next thing he knew he landed with a thump. "Ooomp!" he grunted.

Charlotte laughed so hard, her web began to sway.

"What did I do wrong?" asked the pig, when he recovered from his bump.

"Nothing," said Charlotte. "It was a nice try."

"I think I'll try again," said Wilbur, cheerfully. "I believe what I need is a little piece of string to hold me."

The pig walked out to his yard. "You there, Templeton?" he called. The rat poked his head out from under the trough.

"Got a little piece of string I could borrow?" asked Wilbur. "I need it to spin a web."

"Yes, indeed," replied Templeton, who saved string. "No trouble at all. Anything to oblige." He crept down into his hole, pushed the goose egg out of the way, and returned with an old piece of dirty white string. Wilbur examined it.

"That's just the thing," he said. "Tie one end to my tail, will you, Templeton?"

Wilbur crouched low, with his thin, curly tail toward the rat. Templeton seized the string, passed it around the end of the pig's tail, and tied two half hitches. Charlotte watched in delight. Like Fern, she was truly fond of Wilbur, whose smelly pen and stale food attracted the flies that she needed, and she was proud to see that he was not a quitter and was willing to try again to spin a web.

While the rat and the spider and the little girl watched, Wilbur climbed again to the top of the manure pile, full of energy and hope.

"Everybody watch!" he cried. And summoning all his strength, he threw himself into the air, headfirst. The string trailed behind him. But as he had neglected to fasten the other end to anything, it didn't really do any good, and Wilbur landed with a thud, crushed and hurt. Tears came to his eyes. Templeton grinned. Charlotte just sat quietly. After a bit she spoke.

"You can't spin a web, Wilbur, and I advise you to put the idea out of your mind. You lack two things needed for spinning a web."

"What are they?" asked Wilbur, sadly.

"You lack a set of spinnerets, and you lack know-how. But cheer up, you don't need a web. Zuckerman supplies you with three big meals a day. Why should you worry about trapping food?"

Wilbur sighed. "You're ever so much cleverer and brighter than I am, Charlotte. I guess I was just trying to show off. Serves me right."

Templeton untied his string and took it back to his home. Charlotte returned to her weaving.

"You needn't feel too badly, Wilbur," she said. "Not many creatures can spin webs. Even men aren't as good at it as spiders, although they *think* they're pretty good, and they'll *try* anything. Did you ever hear of the Queensborough Bridge?"

Wilbur shook his head. "Is it a web?"

"Sort of," replied Charlotte. "But do you know how long it took men to build it? Eight whole years. My goodness, I would have starved to death waiting that long. I can make a web in a single evening."

"What do people catch in the Queensborough Bridge—bugs?" asked Wilbur.

"No," said Charlotte. "They don't catch anything. They just keep trotting back and forth across the bridge thinking there is something better on the other side. If they'd hang head-down at the top of the thing and wait quietly, maybe something good would come along. But no—with men it's rush, rush, rush, every minute. I'm glad I'm a sedentary spider."

"What does sedentary mean?" asked Wilbur.

"Means I sit still a good part of the time and don't go wandering all over creation. I know a good thing when I see it, and my web is a good thing. I stay put and wait for what comes. Gives me a chance to think."

"Well, I'm sort of sedentary myself, I guess," said the pig. "I have to hang around here whether I want to or not. You know where I'd really like to be this evening?"

"Where?"

"In a forest looking for beechnuts and truffles and delectable roots, pushing leaves aside with my wonderful strong nose, searching and sniffing along the ground, smelling, smelling, smelling . . ."

"You smell just the way you are," remarked a lamb who had just walked in. "I can smell you from here. You're the smelliest creature in the place."

Wilbur hung his head. His eyes grew wet with tears. Charlotte noticed his embarrassment and she spoke sharply to the lamb.

"Let Wilbur alone!" she said. "He has a perfect right to smell, considering his surroundings. You're no bundle of sweet peas yourself. Furthermore, you are interrupting a very pleasant conversation. What were we talking about, Wilbur, when we were so rudely interrupted?"

"Oh, I don't remember," said Wilbur. "It doesn't make any difference. Let's not talk any more for a while, Charlotte. I'm getting sleepy. You go ahead and finish fixing your web and I'll just lie here and watch you. It's a lovely evening." Wilbur stretched out on his side.

Twilight settled over Zuckerman's barn, and a feeling of peace.

Think Critically

1. What is Wilbur like? How do you know?
   MAKE INFERENCES

2. How does Charlotte feel as she watches Wilbur try to spin a web? CHARACTER'S EMOTIONS

3. If you had been watching Wilbur as he tried to spin a web, would you have told him that it was impossible? Why or why not? EXPRESS PERSONAL OPINIONS

4. How can you tell that the author thinks people rush too much? DRAW CONCLUSIONS

5. **WRITE** Describe a time when you tried to do something new with the help of others.
   EXTENDED-RESPONSE

E. B. White

E. B. White couldn't remember a time in his life when he wasn't busy writing. He said he always wanted to put his thoughts down on paper, and since he couldn't draw, he wrote words instead. He first worked as a newspaper reporter. Then he began writing articles for a magazine.

The children in his family loved the stories he told, so he decided to turn the stories into books. The first book was *Stuart Little*. The second book was *Charlotte's Web*. E. B. White got the idea for this story when he was feeding the pig on his farm in Maine. Around the same time, he had been watching a big gray spider at her work and was amazed by how clever she was at spinning.

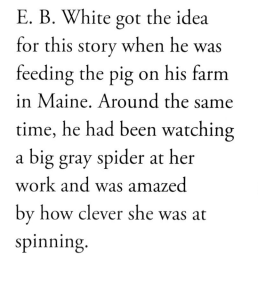

Garth Williams

When he was young, Garth Williams lived on a farm in New Jersey. He loved riding on the tractor with the farmer and watching him milk the cows. When he was ten, his family moved to England, where he went to school.

Both of his parents were artists, so Garth Williams decided to become an artist, too. He said, "Everybody in my house was either painting or drawing, so I thought there was nothing else to do in life but make pictures." He illustrated more than eighty children's books, including *Charlotte's Web,* and wrote and illustrated several books of his own.

 www.harcourtschool.com/storytown

Moths and butterflies

Expository Nonfiction

CATERPILLARS SPIN WEBS, TOO!

by Shane F. McEvey

Spiders aren't the only living things that make and use silk webs. Caterpillars spin webs, too!

CATERPILLARS

Sometimes a number of caterpillars will live together in a web of silk that they all weave together. When they make their web, (left) the caterpillars weave irritating hairs from their bodies into it. This helps to protect the caterpillars from predators.

Case moth caterpillars build cases made of silk and sticks to live in. They carry the case with them wherever they go (right). When something attacks them, they hide inside.

case moth caterpillar ▶

314

COCOONS

Some caterpillars build a cocoon before they become a pupa. The cocoon protects the pupa while it is turning into an adult. Cocoons can be different shapes and sizes but are always made of silk. Sometimes caterpillars will build leaves and hairs into their cocoons for extra protection.

When this white-stemmed gum moth caterpillar made its cocoon (right), it wove hairs from its body into the silk. These hairs hurt to touch. This helps protect the pupa inside the cocoon.

MILLIONS OF MONARCHS

A Monarch caterpillar doesn't build a cocoon to protect itself. It forms a chrysalis instead. Before the caterpillar can form a chrysalis, it needs to use silk. The caterpillar spins a silk "button" to fasten its chrysalis to a twig. After two weeks, a beautiful butterfly comes out of the chrysalis.

Monarchs can be found during the spring and summer in most areas of the United States. They live in warmer states, such as California, Texas, and Florida year-round.

Monarchs

Connections

Comparing Texts

1. Think about the reason that caterpillars spin webs and the reason that spiders spin webs. How are they alike? How are they different?

2. Would you like to have a friend like Charlotte? Explain.

3. Could the events in "Charlotte's Web" happen in real life? How do you know?

Vocabulary Review

Rate a Situation

Work with a partner. Take turns reading aloud each sentence and pointing to the spot on the word line that shows how friendly or unfriendly the action is. Discuss your answers.

friendly ————————————————— unfriendly

- **boasting** about winning a race
- wanting to **oblige** when someone asks for help
- **summoning** you when it is your turn to play
- acting as a **nuisance** when you are trying to work

summoning

nuisance

sedentary

oblige

boasting

sway

Fluency Practice

Readers' Theater

Meet with a small group, and choose a section of "Charlotte's Web" to perform as Readers' Theater. Select roles, including a narrator. Notice the punctuation so that you can read with the correct expression. Ask the audience for feedback after your reading.

Writing

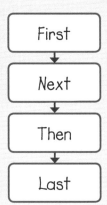

My Writing Checklist

Writing Trait ➤ Word Choice

✓ I use a sequence chart to plan my writing.

✓ I use accurate words to describe events and feelings.

Write a Diary Entry

Write a diary entry from the point of view of one of the characters in "Charlotte's Web." Describe what happens and how the character feels afterward. Use a sequence chart to help you plan your entry.

First
↓
Next
↓
Then
↓
Last

Reading-Writing Connection

Research Report

Before writing a **research report**, a writer gathers information, takes notes, and makes an outline. I wrote this report about silk after reading "Charlotte's Web" and "Caterpillars Spin Webs, Too!"

Student Writing Model

Silk, an Amazing Fiber
by Sarah

Did you know that spiders and silkworms produce a fiber that is one of the strongest in the world? They produce silk, nature's strongest thread. In fact, silk thread is stronger than steel wire of the same size!

Scientists are working to make an artificial silk fiber as strong as a spider's. It could be used to make protective clothing for police officers. It might also be used to connect muscles and broken bones.

Silk is an amazing fiber. It is soft, yet very strong. Most importantly, it may be used to save lives one day soon.

Writing Trait

WORD CHOICE
Use exact words and correct terms.

Writing Trait

IDEAS
Keep ideas in focus. Detail sentences give facts that support the main idea.

Here's how I write a research report.

1. **I think about a topic I want to learn about. Sometimes I discover this topic by chance when I read a book. I may have questions I want answered.**

How strong is silk?
Can people produce silk?
What are some uses for silk?

2. **I narrow my topic if it is too broad. It would be difficult to write one report on all spiders and caterpillars, so I have narrowed it to silk.**

3. **I visit a library and read about my topic in books and magazines. Sometimes I use a computer to find information. I write notes on note cards.**

How strong is silk?

• the strongest fiber in the world

• stronger than steel wire of the same size

4. I organize my information. I use my notes to write an outline. An outline shows the order of main ideas and details. The details give facts.

> Silk
>
> I.   How strong is silk?
>   A. the strongest fiber in the world
>   B. stronger than steel wire
>
> II. What are some possible new uses for silk?
>   A. protective clothing
>   B. help repair bones and muscles
>
> III. Closing
>   A. Silk is soft yet strong.
>   B. It will provide new ways to help people.

5. I write a draft of my research report. I look over my draft and make changes. I add a title that tells what my report is about.

Here is a checklist I use when I write a research report. You can use it, too.

Checklist for Writing a Research Report

☐ My report has an underlined title that tells my reader what it is about.

☐ My report gives facts about one topic.

☐ Each paragraph tells one main idea.

☐ The detail sentences in each paragraph tell facts about the main idea.

☐ I begin my report in an interesting way.

☐ My report follows an order that makes sense.

☐ I use exact words and correct terms to help my reader understand the facts.

Big Idea
Expository nonfiction includes information that helps a reader make inferences about the topic.

Enduring Understanding
The facts in expository nonfiction will lead a reader to make inferences about the selection.

Essential Question
How do readers make inferences?

Spelling Words

Words with V/V Syllable Pattern

lion	piano
dial	fluid
idea	video
neon	loyal
science	stereo
area	pliers
radio	create
quiet	

Challenge

cereal	reality
triumph	scientific
poetry	

Fluency

Punctuation

Robust Vocabulary

- justice
- task
- prey
- shallow
- strands
- social
- spiral
- reels
- elaborate
- inventive

Comprehension

- Make Inferences
- Ask Questions

Phonics

Words with V/V Syllable Pattern

Writing

- Explanation
- Word Choice

Lesson 27

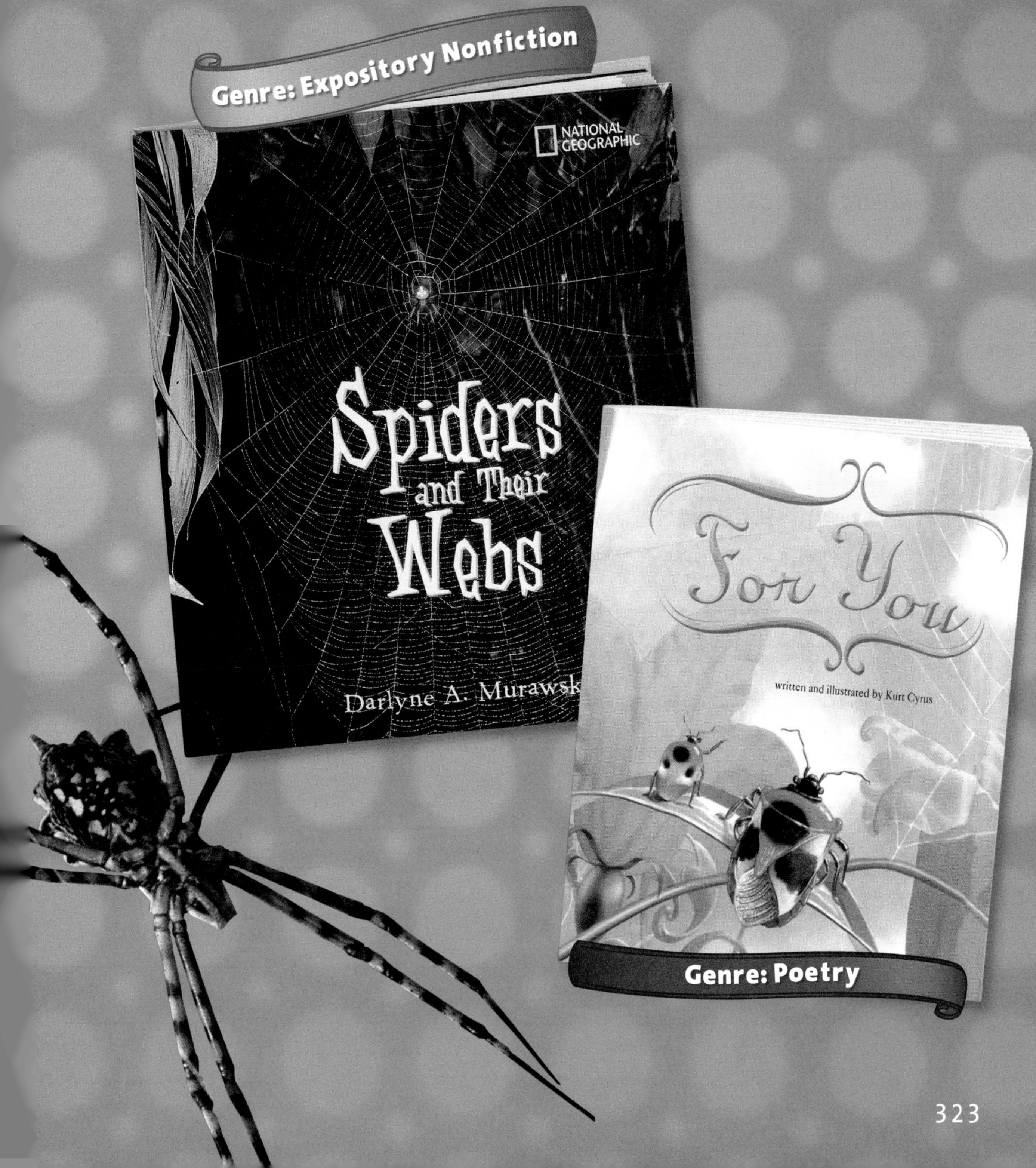
Genre: Expository Nonfiction
NATIONAL GEOGRAPHIC
Spiders and Their Webs
Darlyne A. Murawsk
For You
written and illustrated by Kurt Cyrus
Genre: Poetry

Focus Skill

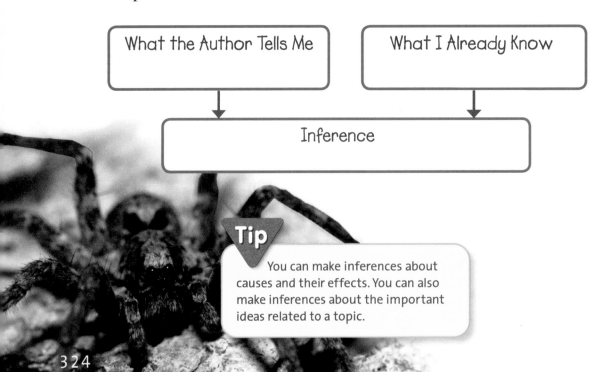 Make Inferences

Remember that authors do not always tell readers everything they want them to know about a topic. When you add what you already know to what an author has told you, you **make inferences.**

- First, look for clues in what the author tells you.
- Next, think about what you already know.
- Then, use what the author tells you and what you know to make inferences.

Making inferences can help you better understand the important ideas in a selection.

What the Author Tells Me	What I Already Know

Inference

Tip

You can make inferences about causes and their effects. You can also make inferences about the important ideas related to a topic.

Read the article. Then use the chart to make an inference about spiders.

Many kinds of spiders live in Florida. Since they eat insects, they can find plenty of food in this part of the world. Spiders have many ways of catching their prey. Some use webs. Wolf spiders and jumping spiders hunt for their food.

All spiders have good eyesight. Jumping spiders have three rows of eyes. Wolf spiders also use vibrations of the ground to tell them when insects are near.

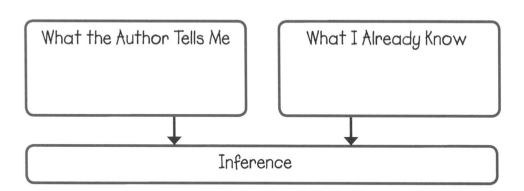

What the Author Tells Me	What I Already Know

Inference

Try This!

Look back at this passage. What inference can you make about insects in Florida?

 www.harcourtschool.com/storytown

Vocabulary

Build Robust Vocabulary

prey

shallow

strands

social

spiral

reels

A Florida Wildlife Tour

The scrub lands of Florida are dry. Their climate is perfect for lizards, spiders, gopher tortoises, and mice. The Florida scrub lizard hunts **prey** such as ants, beetles, and spiders. Wolf spiders are hunters, too. They hide in **shallow** burrows or under dry leaves. Gopher tortoises eat many kinds of plants. They share long tunnels with other animals.

When the gopher tortoise leaves its tunnel, mice might move in. The mice will line their nests with **strands** of Spanish moss.

You can see **social** animals such as wood storks or river otters on a visit to one of Florida's freshwater swamps. Wood storks live in colonies and wade in the water. River otters are playful. They rest on the water's banks and dive in to catch fish.

Many snakes live in the swamps. The venomous water moccasin hunts rabbits. It curls into a **spiral** shape when it rests.

river otter

This man **reels** in a fish.

 www.harcourtschool.com/storytown

Word Champion

Your mission this week is to use the Vocabulary Words in conversation with friends and family. For example, describe places where you might find a spiral pattern. Write in your vocabulary journal the sentences you used that had Vocabulary Words.

Expository Nonfiction

Genre Study

Expository nonfiction explains information and ideas. Look for

- charts that give additional information.
- facts and details that help you build an understanding of a topic.

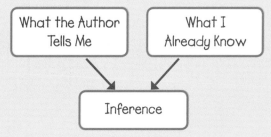

| What the Author Tells Me | What I Already Know |

↓ Inference ↓

Comprehension Strategy

Ask questions as you read to help you better understand the text.

Spiders
and Their
Webs

by Darlyne A. Murawski

Introduction

You can find spider webs just about everywhere you look—in forests, deserts, gardens, even underwater. About 13,000 of the 38,000 known species of spiders make webs to capture insects and other small prey.

Spider webs are made of silk threads. Young and female spiders are usually the web builders. Spider silk is liquid when it is inside glands in the spider's abdomen. It becomes threadlike as it is drawn out of tiny openings in the spinnerets on the bottom of the spider's abdomen. A thread of spider silk is stronger than a thread of steel of the same thickness. Some silk is stretchy, like a rubber band. Some is sticky. In fact, spiders can make as many as seven different kinds of silk. Each kind is used for a different purpose, such as making egg cases or wrapping prey, like the Argiope (far right).

When an insect gets stuck in the threads, the spider attacks. To keep their prey from escaping, spiders inject venom from their fangs. They may also wrap prey tightly in silk. Most spiders have teeth to chew an insect's hard exoskeleton. They spit up juices that turn the prey's insides to liquid so they can drink it.

Spiders deserve our respect. They control insect populations and, in turn, become food for birds and many other animals. Although most spiders aren't harmful to us, a few species deliver a bite that can be painful or even deadly. With spiders, it's best for their safety and ours to LOOK BUT DON'T TOUCH.

Golden Orb Weaver

This huge spider (photograph, right) is a golden orb weaver. That tiny spider with her is her mate! Her web can be three feet wide or larger. It is strong enough to last for several days. This spider can choose the color of silk she makes to spin her webs: gold for webs in sunny places; white for webs in shady places. What looks like drops of water on the web (small photograph, bottom right) are really glue drops. When an insect, like the bee in the art above, flies into the web, it gets stuck in a sticky mess. The spider runs out and bites it with her long fangs. She can eat the insect right away or wrap it in silk and store it in her web for later.

DID YOU KNOW? Spiders know if a visitor is the right size to eat by how much the web shakes when it lands. Luckily, male golden orb weavers are too small to be mistaken for food.

SPIDER FACTS

🕷 **Common names:** golden orb weaver, golden silk spider, banana spider

🕷 **Habitats:** forests and clearings in northern South America, in Central America, and in the southern United States (mainly Florida and Texas)

🕷 **Food:** mainly a variety of flying insects, such as moths, flies, and bees, but has also been known to eat small birds and frogs

🕷 **Body size:** 24 to 40 mm (adult females; males are much smaller)

24 - 40 mm

0	25	50 millimeters
0	1	2 inches

SPIDER FACTS

🕷 **Common name:** Hawaiian happy-faced spider

🕷 **Habitats:** underside of leaves in Hawaiian wet forests, from Oahu to the big island of Hawaii

🕷 **Food:** small insects, such as young leafhoppers and fruit flies

🕷 **Body size:** up to 5 mm (adult females; males are smaller)

5 mm
▬

0				25				50	millimeters

0		1		2	inches

Hawaiian
Happy-Faced Spider

You have to use a magnifying glass to see this tiny yellow spider with the big grin on her abdomen. She makes a messy little web in a shallow dip on the underside of a leaf. The spider uses her web to protect her eggs and to store food. When a small insect visits her leaf, she springs into action. With her hind legs, she pulls silk from her spinnerets and tosses it over her prey. Then, she reels it in. After she wraps her meal in silk, she tucks it in the web next to her eggs. When she gets hungry, she'll eat it. After her eggs hatch, she'll use the web as a nursery and find food for her babies for a few months.

 DID YOU KNOW? Not all happy-faced spiders have a smiley-face pattern on their abdomens. Some have other expressions or just an abstract design.

Water Spider

This kind of spider lives underwater, but it needs air to breathe. To solve this problem, it builds an air-bubble house. First it attaches strands of silk to the leaves and stems of water plants. Then it fills the space with a netlike web. The spider makes several trips to the surface. Each time, a bubble of air sticks to its hairy abdomen. The spider carries the air bubbles back to its web and brushes them off. The air makes the web swell up like a balloon. The spider swims outside its house to catch its food, then drags it inside to eat.

DID YOU KNOW? Water spiders must swim to the surface often to get new air for their webs. The new air is rich in oxygen, which the spider needs to breathe.

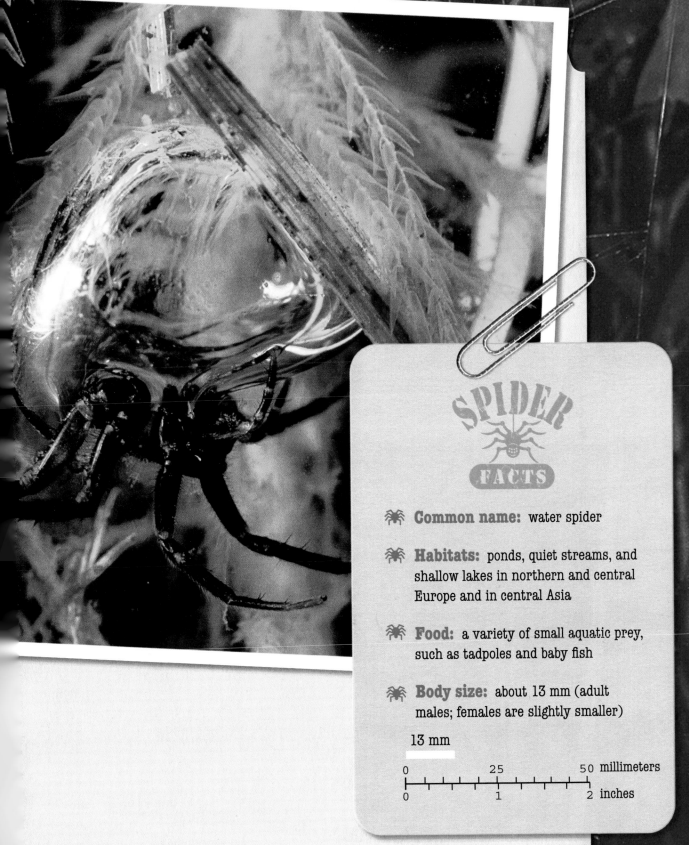

SPIDER
FACTS

🕷 **Common name:** water spider

🕷 **Habitats:** ponds, quiet streams, and shallow lakes in northern and central Europe and in central Asia

🕷 **Food:** a variety of small aquatic prey, such as tadpoles and baby fish

🕷 **Body size:** about 13 mm (adult males; females are slightly smaller)

13 mm

0	25	50 millimeters
0	1	2 inches

SPIDER FACTS

🕷 **Common name:** social spider

🕷 **Habitats:** along waterways and in undergrowth of rain forests from Panama south to Brazil

🕷 **Food:** insects of various sizes, including beetles, butterflies, katydids, dragonflies, and wasps

🕷 **Body size:** 5mm (adult females; males are slightly smaller)

5 mm

| 0 | | 25 | | 50 | millimeters |
| 0 | | 1 | | 2 | inches |

Social Spiders

Some spiders live together in groups. They are called social spiders. Thousands of these spiders work together to make a web that can be as big as a garbage truck! The web has a sheet of silk across the bottom. Lots of long lines attach the sheet to the branches of trees and shrubs, as shown in the art above. These lines "trip" flying insects. They fall down and are caught in the sheet. The tiny spiders you see in the photograph (left) are busy attacking a katydid that flew into their web. By working together, social spiders can catch and eat insects that are many times larger than they are.

DID YOU KNOW? Instead of making a new web when it gets damaged or dirty, these spiders work together to repair and clean the one they have.

Ray Spider

The ray spider (right) makes an orb web that it uses like a slingshot to snag a meal. With its front legs, the spider pulls on a silk thread that draws the web back (Step 1). When the spider senses food is near, it loosens its grip on the thread. The web springs out and catches the insect in the sticky, spiral threads (Step 2). Then the spider runs across the web and grabs its prey. Special hairs and claws on the spider's feet keep it from getting stuck in its own web. This spider can use its web a few times before it has to build a new one.

Step 1

Step 2

DID YOU KNOW? You can trick this spider by rubbing your thumb against your fingertips under its web. Sensing something is near, the spider will release its web.

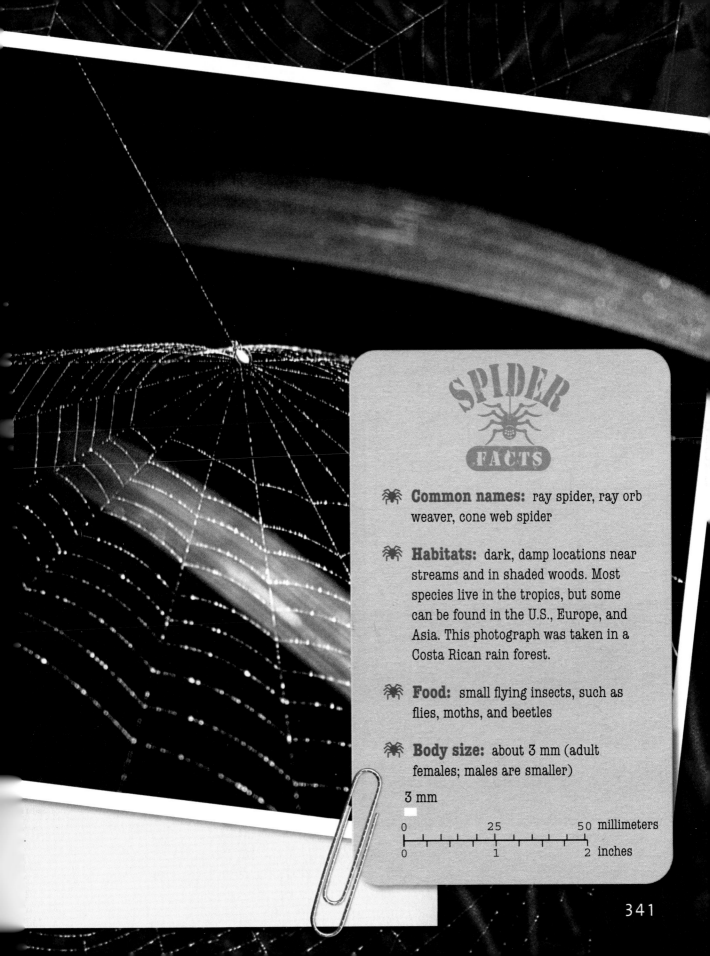

SPIDER FACTS

🕷 **Common names:** ray spider, ray orb weaver, cone web spider

🕷 **Habitats:** dark, damp locations near streams and in shaded woods. Most species live in the tropics, but some can be found in the U.S., Europe, and Asia. This photograph was taken in a Costa Rican rain forest.

🕷 **Food:** small flying insects, such as flies, moths, and beetles

🕷 **Body size:** about 3 mm (adult females; males are smaller)

3 mm

0	25	50	millimeters
0	1	2	inches

341

SPIDER FACTS

🕷 **Common names:** cobweb spider, comb-footed spider, gumfoot spider

🕷 **Habitats:** nooks and crannies in vegetation, under rocks and around buildings

🕷 **Food:** small crawling and flying insects, such as flies

🕷 **Body size:** 2 to 3mm (adult females; males are slightly smaller)

3 mm

```
0          25         50  millimeters
|--|--|--|--|--|--|--|--|--|--|
0            1          2  inches
```

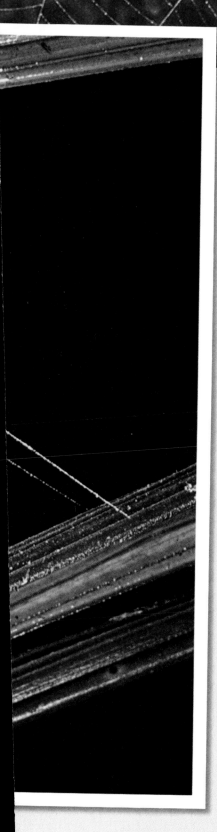

Cobweb
Spider

The spider that made this messy-looking web (photograph, left) is called a cobweb spider. That red dot in the middle is the spider hanging upside-down. It's waiting for a meal. It traps insects with silk threads attached to the lower leaf. They are sticky near the bottom. When an ant or some other kind of small insect touches one of these threads, it gets stuck. The line breaks away from the leaf. Like a yo-yo, it springs up, carrying the insect toward the spider. The spider flings more silk around the insect to make sure it can't get away. Then the spider delivers a deadly bite and sucks its prey dry.

 DID YOU KNOW? Cobweb spiders are some of the easiest spiders to find. Chances are you have some in your house or in your garage.

Think
Critically

① How can you tell that many spiders use webs to survive? 🌀 MAKE INFERENCES

② What does the water spider do first to build its air-bubble house? SEQUENCE

③ What did you learn about spiders that surprised you? EXPRESS PERSONAL OPINIONS

④ How can you tell that the author wants people to be careful around spiders? DRAW CONCLUSIONS

⑤ **WRITE** Choose your favorite web from "Spiders and Their Webs." Use details from the selection to describe your favorite web to someone who has never seen one. ✏ SHORT RESPONSE

Meet the Author and Photographer
Darlyne A. Murawski

Darlyne Murawski loves nature and has traveled all over the world taking pictures of small animals, insects, and marine life. She spent many years studying tropical plants and butterflies.

Darlyne Murawski says she hopes her books will help children become more interested in exploring the world of nature. She also writes articles about nature topics for magazines.

www.harcourtschool.com/storytown

For You

written and illustrated by Kurt Cyrus

Poetry

"Mama, hey Mama Bug, look overhead!
Why is the sky full of silvery thread?"
  "It's there for whoever—for me and for you;
  It's there for us *all*, Bugaboo."

"Mama, hey Mama! Oh, isn't it grand?
A silvery web waving over the land!"
  "It waves at the butterflies up in the blue,
  And also at *you*, Bugaboo."

"Mama, that fellow all covered with fuzz—
Why is he winking, the way that he does?"
  "For houseflies, and horseflies, and hover flies, too—
And *you*, Bugaboo. And for you."

"Mama, he's rubbing his big fuzzy gut.
Fuzzy looks hungry, but hungry for what?"
  "For anyone. Everyone. Who knows who?
For you, Bugaboo. For you."

written and illustrated by Kurt Cyrus

BOINK!

Connections

Comparing Texts

1. How does reading "Spiders and Their Webs" help you understand the poem "For You"?

2. Would you like to be a scientist who studies spiders? Explain your reasons.

3. Why might some people think that spiders are helpful?

Vocabulary Review

Word Webs

With a partner, create word webs for two Vocabulary Words. Put a Vocabulary Word in the center of each web. Then write words that are related to the Vocabulary Word in the web. Share your word webs with your partner.

prey

shallow

strands

social

spiral

reels

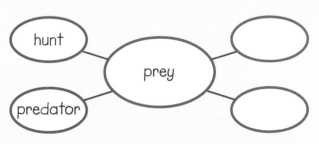

Fluency Practice

Repeated Reading

Choose a section from "Spiders and Their Webs" and read it. Pay attention to commas and end marks so you know when to pause. Then use a stopwatch to time a second reading. Set a goal for a better time. Keep reading until you meet the goal with few or no errors.

Writing

Write a Poem

Write a poem about a spider from "Spiders and Their Webs." The poem does not need to rhyme. Compare the spider and its web to something else. Use a word web to help you plan your ideas. Read the poem aloud to a partner.

My Writing Checklist

Writing Trait → Word Choice

✔ I use a web to brainstorm words for my poem.

✔ I use everyday words that will be familiar to my audience.

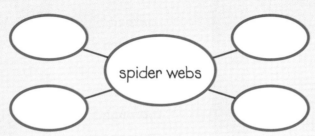

spider webs

Big 💡 Idea
Realistic fiction presents fictional text as if it really occurred.

Enduring ❗ Understanding
Readers can predict what will happen in a story by using information they already know and recalling details from the story.

Essential ❓ Question
How do readers make predictions about the story?

Spelling Words
Words with Suffixes:
-able, -ible, -less, -ous

doable	flexible
famous	washable
careless	helpless
various	terrible
endless	valuable
reliable	dangerous
nervous	powerless
useless	

Challenge

suitable	responsible
restlessly	remarkable
countless	

Fluency
Intonation

Robust Vocabulary
humor
abroad
sprinkled
expand
erupt
thorough
deliberation
grainy
preparation
gimmick

Comprehension
 Make Predictions

 Monitor Comprehension: Read Ahead

Phonics
Words with Suffixes:
-able, -ible, -less, -ous

✏️ Writing
• Description
• Ideas

Lesson 28

Genre: Realistic Fiction

The
Science
Fair

by
Susan
Wojciechowski

illustrated by
Susanna
Natti

Advice from
Dr. Fix-It

Genre: E-mail

Phonics Skill

Words with -*able*, -*ible*, -*less*, and -*ous*

When you read long words, look for suffixes that you know. A suffix is a word part that is added to the end of a word and changes or adds to its meaning. Look at these suffixes and their meanings.

Suffix	Meaning of Suffix	Word
-able	capable of	value + able = valuable
-ible	capable of	flex + ible = flexible
-less	without	end + less = endless
-ous	full of	mystery + ous = mysterious

Read the sentences. Use the meaning of the suffix to help you define each underlined word. Use a dictionary to check the meanings.

- I used a <u>colorless</u> liquid in my experiment.
- You need to be <u>sensible</u> and follow safety rules when you do science experiments.
- Wear <u>comfortable</u> shoes when you walk around the science fair.
- The experiment is <u>worthless</u> if you skip a step.
- The rocket experiment was <u>marvelous</u>.
- Who is <u>responsible</u> for planning the science fair?

Try This!

Look up the word *inflatable* in a dictionary. Write a sentence using the word to show its meaning. Circle the suffix in *inflatable*.

 www.harcourtschool.com/reading

Vocabulary

Build Robust Vocabulary

sprinkled

expand

erupt

thorough

deliberation

grainy

Science in the Kitchen

Monday, April 24

My teacher asked us to study science at home while we cooked. Today, my dad helped me bake volcano biscuits. We mixed baking powder, flour, salt, butter, and milk. Then we spooned piles of the mixture onto a baking sheet and shaped them into cone shapes. Finally, we **sprinkled** nuts on top and put the baking sheet into the oven.

When the biscuits were done, I saw that they had risen. When the baking powder mixed with the milk, it caused the biscuits to **expand**. It was fun to imagine that our volcano biscuits could **erupt** at any time!

Tuesday, April 25

Today, Dad and I made a **thorough** search in a cookbook. After much **deliberation**, we chose a fudge recipe. We mixed the ingredients and cooked the mixture until its temperature was 234°F. I waited to stir the mixture until it cooled to 110°F. If I stirred it too soon, big crystals would form that would make the fudge **grainy**. Because I waited to stir it, our fudge was tasty and smooth.

 www.harcourtschool.com/storytown

Word Scribe

Your mission this week is to use the Vocabulary Words in your writing. For example, write about a time when a choice you made needed much deliberation. Read your sentences to a classmate.

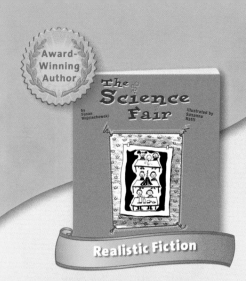

The Science Fair

by Susan Wojciechowski

Illustrated by Suzanne Natti

Realistic Fiction

Genre Study

Realistic fiction is a story with characters and events that are like people and events in real life. Look for

- details that help the reader make predictions.

- a plot with a beginning, a middle, and an end.

Beginning

↓

Middle

↓

End

Comprehension Strategy

Monitor comprehension—Read ahead if something does not make sense to you as you read.

The Science Fair

by
Susan
Wojciechowski

illustrated by
Susanna
Natti

Ms. Babbitt's third-grade class is having a science fair. Beany is a girl in that class who doesn't like science. Her partner, Kevin Gates, is good at science. He came up with two experiments to show that heat makes liquids and gases expand, or get bigger. Beany is proud of herself for figuring out how to show that solids also expand when they are heated.

But Beany is worried that their experiment will not get a good grade. Some of the other students are making glittery posters. Others are going to play music. Kevin insists that all they need is good science. How can they compete without fancy props?

On the day of the science fair, I woke up early, before the alarm went off. I lay in bed hugging Jingle Bell and worrying.

"What if our project is the worst one there?" I said to Jingle Bell. "What if I mess up when I do my part for the judges? What if the judges laugh when they walk away from our table? What if Ms. Babbitt told us that she liked our project just to be nice?" Ms. Babbitt would do something like that. Once I heard my dad tell my mom that Ms. Babbitt does a good job of building self-esteem. When I asked him what that meant, he said she works hard to make us kids feel good about ourselves.

Jingle Bell understood that there was a lot to worry about.

On the bus that morning, I saw that Carol Ann and Stacy were dressed alike. Carol Ann and Stacy didn't seem worried. They were talking nonstop about how much fun the science fair was going to be.

"We're handing out rock candy to everyone who comes to see our project," Carol Ann said. "I bet we win first prize."

"Well, maybe second," said Stacy. "The volcano project sounds really great."

Nathaniel and Montrell's project was about how volcanoes erupt. They were going to build a volcano out of papier-mâché and put something inside that would make it get all bubbly, like a volcano erupting.

Stacy said to me, "Your project is good, too," but I knew she was just doing self-esteem on me.

After lunch we went into the gym. There were three rows of tables with four tables in each row set up at one end of the gym.

"You have a half-hour to set up your projects," Ms. Babbitt said. "And have fun," she added. I felt like throwing up.

Gases, liquids, and solids get bigger when they're heated up. It is Not Magic! It is Science!

The Experiments

Heat makes things get bigger:

A. Gas

B. Liquid

C. Solid

A. Gas (air)

1.

heat

2.

B. Liquid

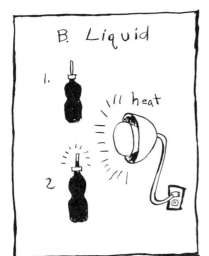

1.

heat

2.

C. Solid

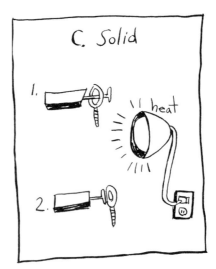

1.

heat

2.

Kevin and I covered our table with a white tablecloth that my mom let us use. It had a big gravy stain in the middle, but she said we could set something on top of the stain so it wouldn't show. We laid out our stuff and a sign. I taped my posters to the front of the table.

When we were finished setting up, I walked around the gym to see what the other teams were doing. When I saw the volcano, I ran back to our table. "Kevin, you should see the volcano. It's huge. Why didn't we think of a volcano?"

Before Kevin could say anything, I ran off to look at other projects, then went back to report to Kevin. "Carol Ann and Stacy have streamers all around the edge of their table. Why didn't we think of that? Should I call my mom to ask if she'll run out and buy us some streamers? She'd do it. I know she would."

"We don't need streamers," said Kevin.

I left our table again, then went back with more news. "Manuel and Boomer are doing a planet project, and they have a black tablecloth with stars all over it. Why didn't we use a cool tablecloth instead of a dumb white one with a gravy stain on it?"

"You need to chill," said Kevin. "Forget about what other people are doing and just—" But before Kevin could finish, I ran off again. In a minute I was back.

"Linda and Elaine have bubbles for their project, big ones!" I said, out of breath. "Everybody loves bubbles. Why didn't we do bubbles?"

"Beany," he said, "could you go get some paper towels in case the red water comes up to the top of the straw and runs over?"

Then I noticed the crowd of kids around the table next to ours. I peeked over. It was Shaleeta and Jessica's project. They had a bunch of big balloons on their table and a plate sprinkled with black pepper. "Oh no," I said to Kevin. "Look at all those balloons! Balloons are even better than bubbles! How come we only have one itsy-bitsy one in our project?"

Shaleeta rubbed a balloon on her arm and then held the balloon a few inches above the plate of pepper. The pepper jumped right off the plate onto the balloon.

"That happens because of static electricity," Shaleeta explained. Everyone said, "Wow." One kid even said, "That's a winner."

My stomach started to hurt. I told Kevin I had to go to Mrs. Facinelli's office to lie down. Mrs. Facinelli is the school nurse. She has *Ranger Rick* magazines we can look at while we try to feel better.

"If I'm not back by the time it's our turn, you go ahead without me," I said. I almost got away, but Kevin grabbed my arm.

"Paper towels," he said.

Parents started to come into the gym and walk from table to table. Teachers from our school brought their classes to see the projects, too. When I saw my mom and dad, I waved to them, and they came over to wish us luck. Kevin said his mom was going to try to get off work early and come, but even though he kept looking toward the door and looking all around the gym, I don't think he saw her.

Then the judges showed up and went from table to table. I started to bite my nails. When they got to the balloon table, I knew we were next. My knees got wobbly.

As the judges walked to our table, Kevin took one last look toward the gym door. He started waving. "She made it," he said. I looked toward the door and saw a woman coming into the gym. She looked out of breath, like she'd been running.

Mr. Shanner said, "Hi, Beany and Kevin. What do we have here?"

"We have a project to show that heat makes things expand, or get bigger," Kevin said.

Then he poked me with his elbow, and I said, "We will now show how heat makes gases expand." Then Kevin did the experiment with the balloon on the bottle and explained everything he was doing as he went along.

Next I said, "We will now show how heat makes liquids expand." Kevin did the bottle and straw experiment and explained it. We did not need paper towels. The red water didn't come up too high, just high enough.

Then it was Kevin's turn to talk. He said, "We will now show how heat makes solids expand." This time I did the experiment, the one with the nail and the eye. When we were finished, Mr. Shanner said, "Hmm." The judges wrote stuff on clipboards and asked us a few questions. They shook our hands and moved on to the next table.

"Why weren't they smiling when they shook our hands?" I asked Kevin. "Why didn't they say *wow* when the water came up the straw? Why did Mr. Shanner say *hmm*? What were they writing on their clipboards?"

Kevin sat down and smiled. "We did a good job," he said.

While we were waiting for the judges to make their decisions, I went over to Carol Ann and Stacy's table and asked how their presentation went.

"Well," said Carol Ann, "I think the judges liked our outfits and the necklaces, but they told us to turn off the music so they could hear us better. Plus, we were supposed to start growing the crystals a few days ago, only we forgot to read the instructions on the box. We didn't do it till this morning, so the crystals are kind of small."

I looked at the fish bowl of water on their table. It had a string going through the water and the crystals were supposed to be growing on the string, but all I could see was a little bit of pink grainy stuff on one part of the string.

"And," Stacy added, "Boomer's mom broke a tooth eating our rock candy."

"How did yours go?" Carol Ann asked me.

"Okay, I guess."

The judges came back into the gym. We all went back to our tables. I crossed my fingers. Ms. Kowalski said, "We were very impressed with the efforts of all the students. We hope they are as proud of themselves as we are of them."

Then Mr. Shanner said, "It was hard for us to choose the three best, but after much deliberation, we have chosen for third place the static electricity experiment. It was creative and educational." Shaleeta and Jessica screamed.

My only hope had been third place. I sighed. I uncrossed my fingers and clapped as they went up to get their certificates and third-place ribbons.

Next, Ms. Kowalski gave the second-place award. It went to the volcano project. "Nathaniel and Montrell's volcano was impressive," she said, "but it was their charts and their explanation of what causes a volcano to erupt that we especially liked. Those were thorough and easy to understand."

After the clapping, Mr. Shanner coughed, then said, "Now, for the first-place project. We felt the winning project was a fine example of real science. It was organized, clear, and complete."

I knew we wouldn't get first place. I started reciting the sevens times tables in my head, just to keep myself from crying. But right at seven times four, Kevin started pushing me out from behind our table.

"Go," he said. "We won."

"We what?"

"We won."

I screamed and jumped up and down. I couldn't believe it!

Kevin and I each got a certificate and a blue ribbon that had FIRST PLACE, SCIENCE FAIR stamped on it in gold letters. Ms. Babbitt hugged us. Then she whispered in my ear, "I knew you could make it work." My mom and dad came up and hugged us. So did Kevin's mom.

"Thanks for coming," I heard Kevin say to her.

"I wouldn't have missed it for anything. I'm just sorry I was late," she said. Then his mom pulled a camera out of her purse. "Say *cheeseburger*," she told Kevin and me.

"Aw, Mom, come on," Kevin said. But he smiled.

Think Critically

1 What do you think Beany will do the next time she enters a science fair? MAKE PREDICTIONS

2 Why are Carol Ann and Stacy's crystals so small? CAUSE/EFFECT

3 Did you think that Beany and Kevin would win first place? Why or why not? EXPRESS PERSONAL OPINIONS

4 How can you tell that the author thinks the content of a science experiment is more important than decorations? DRAW CONCLUSIONS

5 **WRITE** What do you think Beany learned from doing the science experiment? Give examples from the story to support your answer. SHORT-RESPONSE

Meet the Author
Susan Wojciechowski

Susan Wojciechowski had many different jobs before she became a children's book author. She says she discovered writing after her neighbor had a story published in a magazine. She wanted to have her name in a magazine, too!

The author often writes while sitting in a big squishy chair in her living room. Sometimes, an idea will come to her while she is doing the dishes. She says the character for Beany came into her head while she was in bed with the flu.

In her spare time, Susan Wojciechowski likes to do crossword puzzles, read good books, and visit schools. She lives in York, Pennsylvania with her husband and three children.

 www.harcourtschool.com/storytown

Meet the Illustrator
Susanna Natti

When she was only five years old, Susanna Natti liked to copy paintings from her parents' art books. By the time she was eight, she already knew she was going to be an illustrator. Susanna grew up in Gloucester, Massachusetts, where many artists and authors lived. Her mother, too, was an author of children's books.

Susanna Natti has won awards for some of her illustrations. She likes to work in schools because she thinks that art is especially important there. She also enjoys music, sewing, reading, and gardening. Susanna Natti says, "I love to garden and read—NOT garden and WEED!"

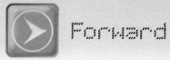

Advice from
Dr. Fix-It

Dr.Fix-It@online.com

From: I.C.Cube@online.com
To: Dr.Fixit@online.com
Date: July 29, 10:27 AM
Subject: Help!

Dear Dr. Fix-It,

I was chilling out in the ice-cube tray when someone grabbed me and put me in a glass. Now I'm out in the sun, and I can't stop melting! Please help!

I. C. Cube

From: Dr.Fixit@online.com
To: I.C.Cube@online.com
Date: July 29, 10:43 AM
Subject: Re: Help!

Dear I.C.,

Don't worry. You're melting because you're made up of tiny particles. In the freezer, they weren't moving much. The sun gave them heat energy. This made them move so much that you couldn't hold your shape!

Best wishes,

Dr. Fix-It

From: I.C.Cube@online.com
To: Dr.Fixit@online.com
Date: July 29, 11:32 AM
Subject: What Now?

Dear Dr. Fix-It,

Life as a liquid is so much fun! Some shade would be nice, though. I am getting really hot out here. What's going to happen to me next?

Thank you,

I.C. Cube

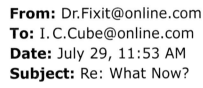

From: Dr.Fixit@online.com
To: I.C.Cube@online.com
Date: July 29, 11:53 AM
Subject: Re: What Now?

Dear I.C.,

If you stay in the sun, your particles will keep moving faster. They will get enough heat energy to break apart and leave the glass. You'll change from a liquid to a gas. This is called evaporation.

We won't see you then, but don't worry. You'll just have changed forms!

Best wishes,

Dr. Fix-It

Connections

Comparing Texts

1. Would Dr. Fix-it like Kevin and Beany's experiment? Explain.

2. Would you like to be Beany's science partner? Why or why not?

3. Why are science fairs important to students in real life?

Vocabulary Review

Word Sort

Work with a partner. Sort the Vocabulary Words into two categories. Decide whether each word describes a *character* or an *object* in "The Science Fair." Take turns explaining why you put each word where you did. Then choose one word from each category and write a sentence that uses both words.

The grainy sand was sprinkled on the paper.

sprinkled

expand

erupt

thorough

deliberation

grainy

Fluency Practice

Readers' Theater

Meet with a small group. Choose a section of "The Science Fair" to read as Readers' Theater. Choose roles from the story, including a narrator. As you read, let your voice rise and fall naturally. Ask for feedback from the audience.

Writing

Write a Letter

Write a letter to the author of "The Science Fair." Tell what you liked about the science fair in the story. Then write what you think the author would like to know about how you study science. Use a chart to help you list your ideas. Include all the parts of a letter in your draft.

My Writing Checklist

Writing Trait ▶ Ideas

✔ I include the date, greeting, body, closing, and signature in my letter.

✔ I give information that would answer questions that the author might have.

Science Fair in Story	How I Study Science

Big Idea

Expository nonfiction uses organizational structure to help a reader make predictions about a topic.

Enduring ! Understanding

Readers use questions and their prior knowledge of a topic to predict.

Essential ? Question

How do the cause-and-effect relationships of a topic help readers make predictions?

Spelling Words

Words with Prefixes:
bi-, non-, over-

overnight	oversee
bicycle	overhead
nonstop	nonfiction
overdue	overcoat
overlook	nonfat
biweekly	overdone
overflow	biplane
nonsense	

Challenge

overtaken	nontoxic
overheat	overboard
nonstick	

Fluency

Intonation

Comprehension

 Make Predictions

 Monitor Comprehension: Read Ahead

Robust Vocabulary

- distinct
- slightly
- rotates
- surface
- steady
- reflects
- appears
- evidence
- infinite
- expansive

Phonics

Words with Prefixes:
bi-, non-, over-

Writing

- Paragraph that Contrasts
- Ideas

Genre: Expository Nonfiction

THE PLANETS

REVISED EDITION

BY GAIL GIBBONS

Jeremy's House

by Lois Simmie
illustrated by Raúl Colón

Genre: Poetry

379

Focus Skill

Make Predictions

As you read, **make predictions** about what will happen next in a story or what you will find out next in an article. To make predictions, use word and picture clues, and think about what you know from reading and from real life.

What I Know	What I Want to Know	What I Learned

After you make a prediction, read on. Continue to revise and confirm your prediction as you read.

Making predictions can help you think about what you are reading and help you remember important details.

Tip

When you read a nonfiction passage, skim the title, the headings, and any illustration captions to help you make predictions about what you will find out.

Use the title and the chart below to make predictions about the article. Then read the article, and use the chart to think about what you learned.

A Journey to Saturn and Beyond

In 1980, the spacecraft *Voyager I* flew past Saturn and sent back images to Earth. For the first time, scientists saw spokes in Saturn's rings. They found three more of Saturn's moons. Later, *Voyager II* traveled even farther and sent back information about Uranus and Neptune.

What I Know	What I Want to Know	What I Learned
Saturn is a planet.		

Try This!

Use the information you read to predict what future space missions will do.

www.harcourtschool.com/storytown

Vocabulary

rotates

surface

steady

reflects

appears

evidence

Here Comes the Sun

Scientists who study the sun have learned that the sun **rotates**. They know that the force of gravity is greater on the sun's **surface** than on Earth's. On the sun, a person would weigh almost thirty times as much as on Earth. However, no one could live on the sun, because the surface is thousands of times hotter than Earth's. Scientists know that powerful solar winds come off the sun and travel through the solar system.

Solar winds are not **steady**. They change in speed and number of particles.

When the solar winds come near Earth, particles in the solar winds interact with particles in the air. Some people may think the night sky **reflects** the colors of the particles. Instead, energy is released that shows up as a flickering light show. This light show **appears** near the North Pole as the northern lights and near the South Pole as the southern lights.

The northern lights can be seen in Alaska.

Scientists have sent balloons up to study these lights and collect **evidence**. They hope to learn more about these strange lights.

 www.harcourtschool.com/reading

Word Detective

Your mission this week is to look for the Vocabulary Words in books about Earth, the sun, the moon, or planets in the solar system. Each time you read a Vocabulary Word, write it in your vocabulary journal. Tell where you found the word.

THE PLANETS

By GAIL GIBBONS

Award-Winning Author

Expository Nonfiction

Genre Study

Expository nonfiction gives information about a topic. Look for

- captions and labels that tell about illustrations.

- facts and details that help you learn about a topic.

What I Know	What I Want to Know	What I Learned

Comprehension Strategy

Monitor comprehension— Read ahead to find information that might help you better understand a passage.

THE PLANETS

by Gail Gibbons

SUN

On a clear night, when stars shine brightly, you might see what looks like another star. But each night it changes position in the star patterns. It is a planet. The word *planet* comes from the Greek word meaning "wanderer."

* STAR

PLANET

A planet is different from a star. People can see a planet because the sun shines on it. A star shines because it is made up of gases that give off light and heat. Our sun is a star. Nearly every star is much bigger than the biggest planet.

The SOLAR SYSTEM includes
the sun and everything
circling around it.

In very early times, people
knew of six planets. They were
Mercury, Venus, Earth, Mars,
Jupiter, and Saturn. These people
named most of the planets after
Roman goddesses and gods.
Later, within the last 200 years,
three more were discovered. They
were Uranus, Neptune, and Pluto.

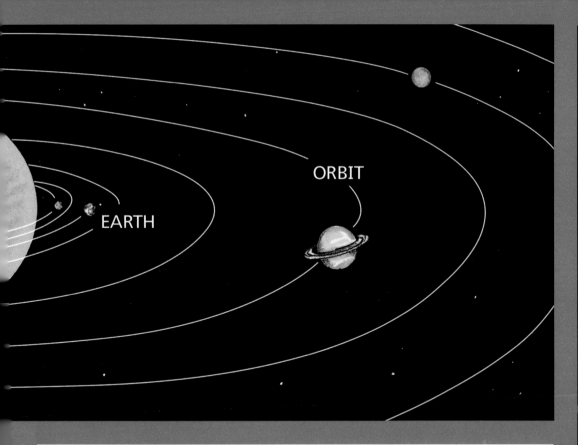

ORBIT

EARTH

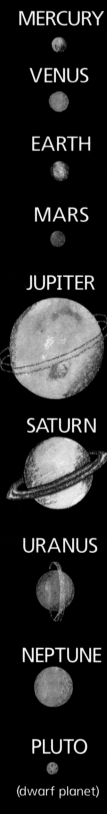

MERCURY

VENUS

EARTH

MARS

JUPITER

SATURN

URANUS

NEPTUNE

PLUTO

(dwarf planet)

Planet Earth is where we live. It is one of the planets that circle the sun. Together they make up the main part of the solar system. The word *solar* means "connected to the sun."

The planets circle around the sun in paths called orbits. The time it takes for a planet to travel around the sun is its year. Each planet's year is different.

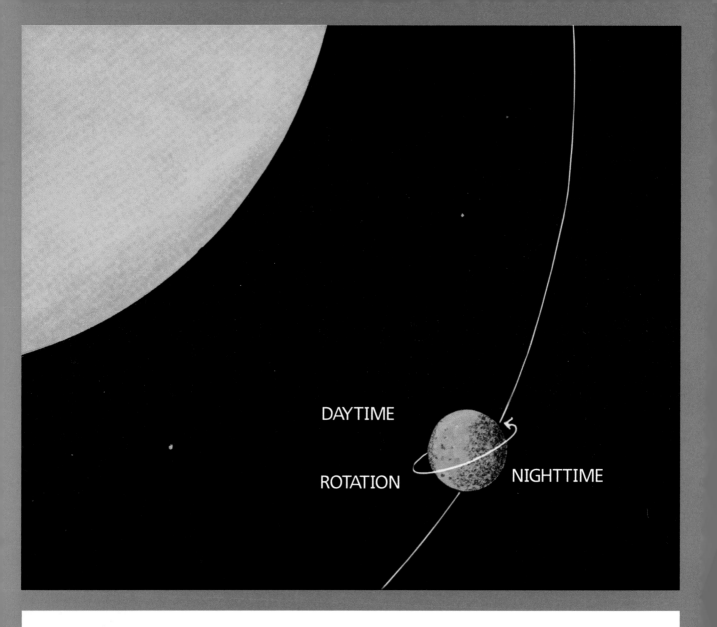

DAYTIME

ROTATION

NIGHTTIME

While a planet is orbiting around the sun, it is moving another way, too. It spins, or **rotates**. The time it takes for a planet to rotate is its day. Each planet's day is different. While a planet is rotating, part of it faces the sun. It is daytime there. On the other side it is nighttime.

People can look up on a clear night and might see Mercury, Venus, Mars, Jupiter, and Saturn. A planet looks like a steady point of light. A star twinkles. A telescope is needed to see Uranus and Neptune. They are very far away from planet Earth.

A TELESCOPE enlarges the image.

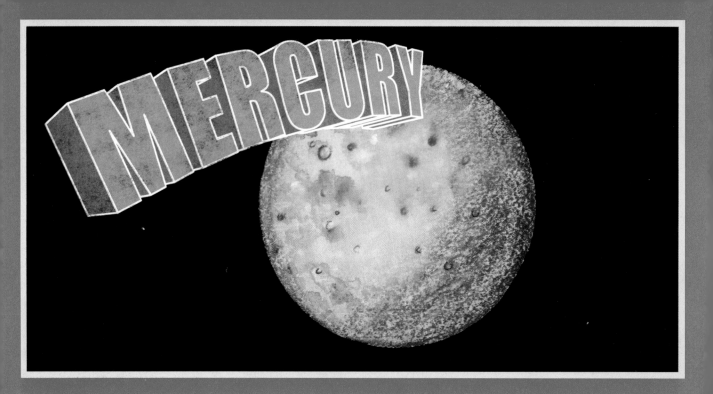

MERCURY

Of the planets, Mercury is the planet closest to the sun. It is about 36 million miles away from the sun. During the day it is extremely hot. During the night it is bitter cold because Mercury doesn't have any atmosphere to keep its heat from escaping.

Mercury is the second smallest planet and is made up of rock and metal. One year on Mercury is only 88 Earth days. That's how long it takes for Mercury to orbit the sun. Mercury rotates very slowly, so its days are very long. A day on Mercury is 59 Earth days.

An ATMOSPHERE is a layer of air.

MERCURY

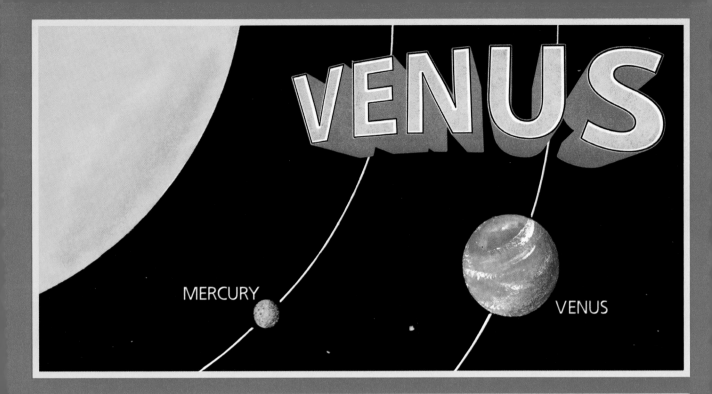

MERCURY

VENUS

Venus is the second planet from the sun. It is usually the brightest object in our sky, other than our sun and moon. At sunrise and sunset, it looks like a big, bright star. It is bright because Venus has a cloud cover that reflects the sunlight. These clouds are made up of gases.

Venus is about 67 million miles away from the sun. It is hot there. Venus is almost the same size as planet Earth. One year on Venus is about 225 Earth days. A day on Venus is about 243 Earth days long because Venus rotates very slowly. On Venus, a day is longer than a year, and a year is shorter than a day.

EARTH

Earth is the third planet from the sun. It is the only planet known to have just the right environment for plants, animals, and people to live in. Earth is 93 million miles from the sun.

Planet Earth has just enough gravity to hold its atmosphere around it. Earth has a moon. The moon causes the tides to change, making them rise and fall. Earth orbits the sun in about 365 days to make an Earth year. It rotates every 24 hours to make an Earth day.

EARTH

MOON

A MOON orbits a planet. It has no light of its own. It reflects sunlight.

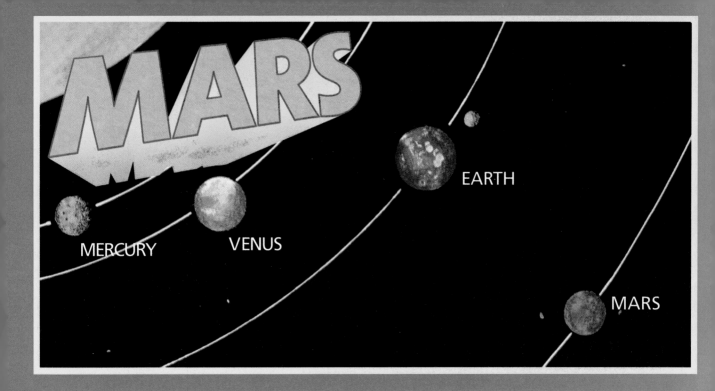

MERCURY

VENUS

EARTH

MARS

Mars is the fourth planet from the sun, about 142 million miles away. People wonder if there was ever life on Mars. Although the surface of Mars is dry now, it once had rivers and perhaps even an ocean. In 2004, the Mars Exploration Rover Mission sent two robotic vehicles to examine the planet's surface. Scientists may still find evidence of life-forms.

MARS ROVER

Astronomers believe that Mars looks red because iron on its surface has been rusted by the planet's thin atmosphere. It is very cold and is a little more than half the size of planet Earth. Mars has two small moons. One year on Mars is about 2 Earth years. A day on Mars is about as long as a day on Earth.

MARS

JUPITER

GREAT RED SPOT

IO
(EYE-o)

GANYMEDE
(GAN-eh-meed)

Jupiter is the fifth planet from the sun. It is about 484 million miles away. It is huge! It is bigger than all the other planets put together and has rings. Jupiter is mostly made up of gases. Some of the gases form a giant red circle called the Great Red Spot.

At least sixty-three moons orbit around planet Jupiter. One moon, Ganymede, is the biggest moon in the solar system. It is bigger than planet Mercury. Another moon, called Io, has many active volcanoes. One Jupiter year is almost 12 Earth years. It has short days, just under 10 Earth hours long.

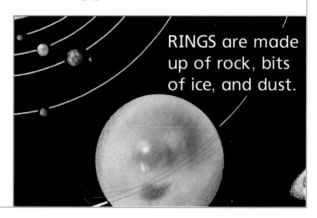

RINGS are made up of rock, bits of ice, and dust.

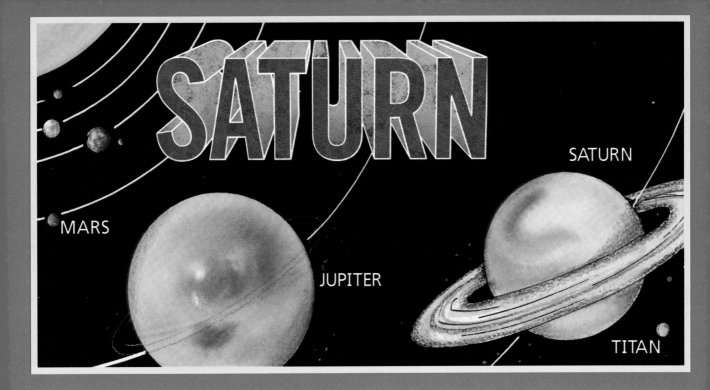

MARS

JUPITER

SATURN

TITAN

Saturn is the sixth farthest planet from the sun, about 887 million miles away. It is the second largest planet. Saturn's hundreds of rings make it look different from the other planets. The rings are made up of ice. Some pieces are as big as houses. On Saturn it is extremely cold.

Saturn has at least forty-six moons. Titan, its largest moon, is the only moon in the solar system with an atmosphere and clouds. It takes almost 30 Earth years for Saturn to orbit the sun. It rotates in about 11 Earth hours.

TITAN

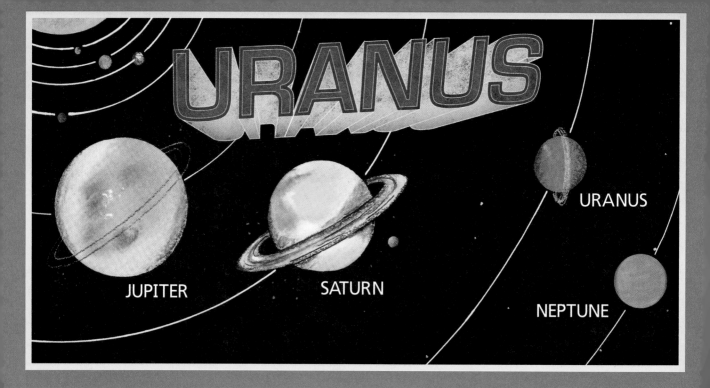

URANUS

JUPITER

SATURN

URANUS

NEPTUNE

Uranus is the seventh planet from the sun. It is about 1.8 billion miles away. It is so far away that from its surface the sun would look tiny. Uranus has ten rings.

Uranus is the third biggest planet, about one-third the size of planet Jupiter. At least twenty-seven moons orbit around it. Planets farther from the sun have longer orbits. They take more time to travel around the sun. For Uranus to make one orbit takes about 84 Earth years. Uranus rotates in about 17 Earth hours.

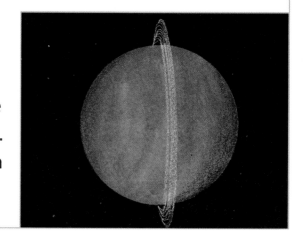

TRITON

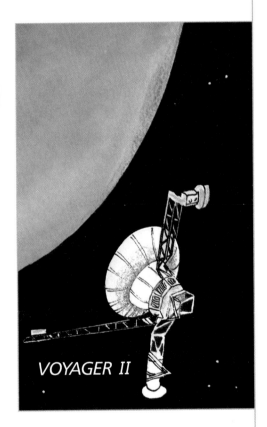

Neptune is the eighth farthest planet from the sun. It is about 2.8 billion miles away. Neptune appears to be blue because of a gas in its atmosphere. It is almost the same size as Uranus.

One of Neptune's thirteen moons, Triton, is about the same size as planet Earth's moon. The spacecraft *Voyager II* visited Neptune in 1989. One Neptune year is 164 Earth years. It rotates in about 16 Earth hours.

VOYAGER II

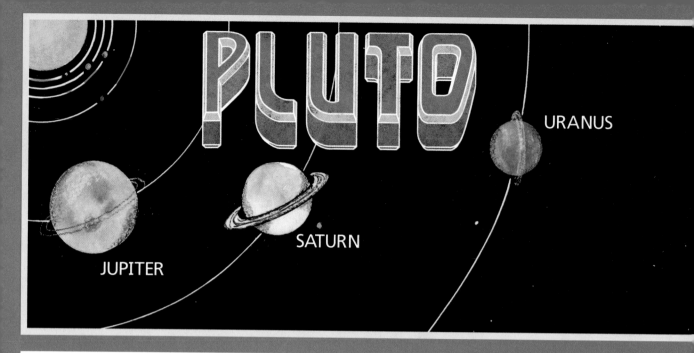

JUPITER

SATURN

URANUS

Until 2006, Pluto was thought to be the ninth and farthest planet from the sun. It is now called a *dwarf planet.* Sometimes its orbit carries it closer to the sun than Neptune. At its farthest, Pluto is about 3.6 billion miles from the sun. It was discovered in 1930.

Pluto is cold and small. It is smaller than Earth's moon. It has one moon called Charon. One year on Pluto is about 248 Earth years long. A day on Pluto is about 6 Earth days long.

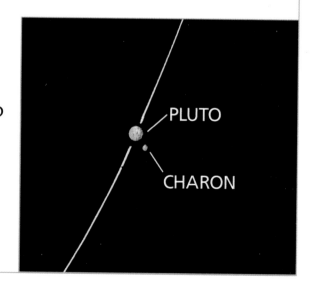

PLUTO

CHARON

NEPTUNE

PLUTO

Here on planet Earth, astronomers search the skies through telescopes. Spacecraft are sent into the solar system and beyond in search of new discoveries.

We are always learning about the planets, the stars, and what lies beyond. It is fun to search the night skies for planets and stars from our planet Earth.

An ASTRONOMER is someone who studies the stars and planets.

 **Mercury**, which is bigger than Earth's moon, has a core of iron.

 **Venus** rotates in the opposite direction of the other eight planets.

 **Earth** is the middle-sized planet. Four of the planets are smaller and four are bigger than planet Earth.

 **Mars** has a very large canyon. It is the biggest in the solar system. It is called Mariner Valley and is thirteen times longer than the Grand Canyon in the United States.

 **Jupiter** is huge! If Jupiter were a big, empty ball, more than one thousand Earths would fill it.

It is very windy on **Saturn**. Around its middle, winds blow ten times stronger than an average hurricane on Earth.

When the spacecraft *Voyager II* flew past **Uranus** in 1986, it had been traveling through space for 9 years.

Neptune is thirty times Earth's distance from the sun. Some astronomers have said that studying Neptune from Earth is like studying a dime a mile away.

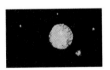
Pluto, now called a dwarf planet, is the only planet that has never been explored by a spacecraft.

1 What clues help readers make predictions about the sequence of "The Planets"? MAKE PREDICTIONS

2 What causes Venus's brightness? CAUSE/EFFECT

3 What information about the planets was most interesting to you? Why? EXPRESS PERSONAL OPINIONS

4 How do you know that the author enjoys learning about space? DRAW CONCLUSIONS

5 **WRITE** Tell about a time when you looked at the nighttime sky. SHORT RESPONSE

GAIL GIBBONS

Question: Did you always want to write and illustrate books?

Answer: Yes! In fact, I put my first book together when I was ten.

Question: How do you choose topics to write about?

Answer: Most of the ideas for my books come from things I love and want to learn more about.

Question: How do you put a book together?

Answer: First, I do all my research. Then I begin to write. Once the words are there, I begin to make pictures to fit the words.

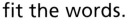 www.harcourtschool.com/storytown

Jeremy's
House

by Lois Simmie
illustrated by Raúl Colón

Poetry

Jeremy's House

Jeremy hasn't a roof on his house
For he likes to look at the stars;
When he lies in his bed
With them all overhead
He imagines that he can see Mars.

Sometimes a thunderstorm lights up the sky
And Jeremy gets soaking wet;
But he says that it's worth it
To lie in his bed
And see folks go past in a jet.

He's counting the stars in the Milky Way,
It's going to take him forever;
But Jeremy's patiently
Counting away
For he knows it's a worthwhile endeavor.

by Lois Simmie
illustrated by Raúl Colón

Connections

Comparing Texts

1. Would you read "The Planets" and "Jeremy's House" to learn information or for enjoyment? Explain your answer.

2. Which planet would you like to learn more about? Explain your choice.

3. Why is it important to know about the planets and the sun?

Vocabulary Review

Word Pairs

Work with a partner. Write each Vocabulary Word on a card. Place the cards face down. Take turns flipping over two cards and writing a sentence that uses both words. Read your sentences to your partner and decide whether the Vocabulary Words are used correctly.

The sun reflects off the surface of the lake.

| rotates |
| surface |
| steady |
| reflects |
| appears |
| evidence |

Fluency Practice

Partner Reading

Meet with a partner. Choose an interesting section from "The Planets." Take turns reading it aloud. Pay attention to how your voice rises and falls. Ask your partner for feedback.

Writing

Write to Compare and Contrast

Choose two planets that you read about. Write to explain how the planets are alike or different. Use a Venn diagram to help you jot down your ideas. In your draft, include accurate details to show how the two planets are alike or different.

My Writing Checklist

Writing Trait ▶ Ideas

✔ I use a Venn diagram to plan my writing.

✔ I add accurate details to support the main idea.

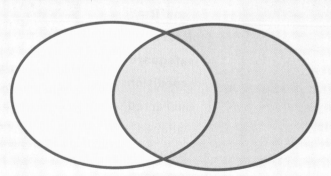

Big Idea
Travel journals use inferences in the characters' dialogue.

Enduring Understanding
Readers make inferences and predictions to understand a selection.

Essential Question
How do readers make predictions from their prior knowledge to make an inference?

Spelling Words

Review

vision	piano
powerless	nonstop
caution	loyal
dangerous	overnight
session	reliable
famous	oversee
fluid	flexible
biplane	

Fluency

Review Punctuation, Intonation

Comprehension

Review
 Make Inferences, Make Predictions

 Ask Questions, Monitor Comprehension: Read Ahead

Robust Vocabulary

- magnify
- observed
- generates
- confirm
- picturesque
- safeguard
- expedition
- uncharted
- aligned
- occur

Phonics

Review
- Words with Suffixes -tion, -sion
- Words with V/V Syllable Pattern
- Words with Suffixes: -able, -ible, -less, -ous
- Words with Prefixes: *bi-, non-, over-*

Writing

- *Review* Word Choice, Ideas
- Revise and Publish

Lesson 30
Theme Review and Vocabulary Builder

Readers' Theater
TRAVEL JOURNAL

Voyage Across the Solar System

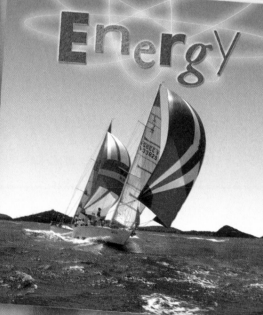

Reading for Information
FUNCTIONAL TEXT

Energy

411

magnify

observed

generates

confirm

picturesque

safeguard

Reading for Fluency

When you read a script aloud,

- let your voice rise and fall as if you were speaking in a conversation.

- pay attention to the different kinds of punctuation.

412

Voyage
Across the
Solar System

Characters

Captain	Doctor	Crew Member 1
Engineer	First Mate	Crew Member 2
	Scientist	

Setting: *Onboard the spaceship* Explorer, *orbiting Pluto*

Captain: This is Space Log entry number 101.

Engineer: We are the crew of the spaceship *Explorer*.

Doctor: This is the record of our travels.

First Mate: We have started our journey back across the solar system, heading toward the sun.

Captain: We're taking a close look at Pluto. For years, Pluto was thought to be the farthest planet from the sun. Now it is called a dwarf planet.

First Mate: Our ship is powered by sunlight. You can barely see the sun this far out in the solar system, so we don't have a lot of power here.

Scientist: I have been studying how much light gets to this part of the solar system. After a thorough investigation, I find that there is less light energy here than there is on Earth.

Doctor: It really is dark out here.

Captain: We have seen Pluto's largest moon, Charon.

Crew Member 1: Captain, why is so little known about Pluto? Don't scientists use telescopes to magnify views?

Captain: It is difficult to study Pluto because it is far from Earth. Even with powerful telescopes, the images of Pluto are grainy and fuzzy.

Crew Member 2: We must be the first humans to fly this close to Pluto!

Doctor: That's correct. Exciting, isn't it?

Everyone: Oh, yes!

Fluency Tip

Pay attention to punctuation, such as commas, as you read. They can be clues for you to take a short pause.

Space Log Entry Number 102

Setting: *Aboard the spaceship* Explorer, *orbiting the planet Uranus*

Captain: This is Space Log entry number 102. We passed Neptune on our way to Uranus.

Engineer: Now that we are closer to the sun, we can collect more solar energy, so we are going faster.

First Mate: A scientist named Galileo first observed Neptune in 1613, but he didn't know it was a planet.

Scientist: Neptune is not solid like Earth. It is a giant blue ball of swirling gases.

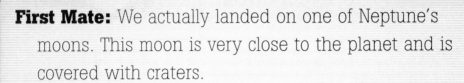

First Mate: We actually landed on one of Neptune's moons. This moon is very close to the planet and is covered with craters.

Captain: Now we are orbiting the planet Uranus. It is between Neptune and Saturn. The sun still looks tiny.

Doctor: The sun is more than a billion miles from us!

Engineer: Now we will head toward Saturn on our way to the biggest planet—Jupiter!

Space Log Entry Number 103

Setting: *Aboard the spaceship* Explorer *on Io*

Captain: This is Space Log entry number 103. We have just managed to pass through the rings of Saturn.

Engineer: We tried to land on Titan, Saturn's gigantic moon, but we got stuck in one of the rings. The pieces of ice that make up the rings were a nuisance!

Captain: We got free, though, and now we're landing near one of the many volcanoes on Io, one of Jupiter's more than sixty moons.

Doctor: It must be very, very hot on the surface! Look at all of those volcanoes!

Crew Member 2: What causes all of this volcanic heat?

Scientist: We believe it is because Io actually wobbles a little as it orbits Jupiter. The wobbling generates heat. This is similar to what happens when you bend a wire coat hanger back and forth. The coat hanger starts to get hot near the bend.

Crew Member 1: So, the wobbling makes Io hot, and that makes the volcanoes erupt.

Scientist: That's what we think.

Engineer: Now we are only 484 million miles from the sun. We are getting more energy from the sun, so we can move a little faster. Soon we'll be landing on Mars.

Fluen

Try to add a stress to the important w sentence as aloud.

Space Log Entry Number 104

Setting: *Aboard the spaceship* Explorer *on the planet Mars*

Captain: This is Space Log entry number 104. We have landed on the Red Planet—Mars!

Doctor: The surface looks as if it has rivers and oceans.

Scientist: It might have had them at one time, but Mars is dry now.

Crew Member 1: Isn't there ice on Mars, though?

Scientist: Yes. There are ice caps at the poles, just as there are on Earth. They're made of frozen water and other materials. It is very likely that there was water once on parts of Mars, but that was many millions, if not billions, of years ago! Solid water is the only form of water that scientists can confirm at this time.

Doctor: Where are all the Martians? I hope they are friendly and social.

Captain: I don't think we'll be meeting any Martians!

Crew Member 2: I wouldn't be so sure of that! Look over there. What is that object on the surface?

First Mate: Oh, that's just one of the Mars Exploration Rovers sent from Earth in 2004. It was designed to run on solar energy, like our spaceship, *Explorer*!

Engineer: Which reminds me, we're close enough to the sun that we can get back to Earth easily.

Doctor: Let's go!

Space Log Entry Number 105

Setting: *Aboard the spaceship* Explorer, *zooming past Earth*

Captain: This is Space Log entry number 105. We have decided not to stop on Earth. The crew of the *Explorer* wants to explore our solar system some more. We are heading toward the next planet, Venus.

Doctor: Earth really looks beautiful from space.

Crew Member 1: With this telescope, I think I can see your home, Doc!

Doctor: Oh, how I miss my home!

First Mate: Don't worry, Doc. We'll get you there soon.

Engineer: In the meantime, I'm going on a space walk outside the ship. I have to fix some of the solar panels on the *Explorer*. Does anyone want to put on a space suit and come along?

Fluency Tip

Think about how the three different kinds of punctuation in this section can help you rea these sentences aloud.

Doctor: I'll go with you!

First Mate: You'll have a picturesque view of Earth's oceans from out there. More than half of Earth is covered by water.

Scientist: Earth is the only planet with all three forms of water: solid, liquid, and gas.

Crew Member 2: What is the big, spiraling white thing near North America?

First Mate: That looks like a big storm system over the Atlantic Ocean.

Scientist: You're right. Clouds that spiral could mean a tropical storm or even a hurricane.

Space Log Entry Number 106

Setting: *Aboard the spaceship* Explorer, *soaring toward Mercury*

Captain: This is Space Log entry number 106. The *Explorer* has just passed the planet Venus. It is getting very hot as we move toward Mercury, the last planet before the sun.

Crew Member 1: I was hoping that we could land the ship on the sun!

Scientist: That would be impossible, because the sun isn't solid. It's made up of burning gases. Besides, the sun is far, far too hot to go near.

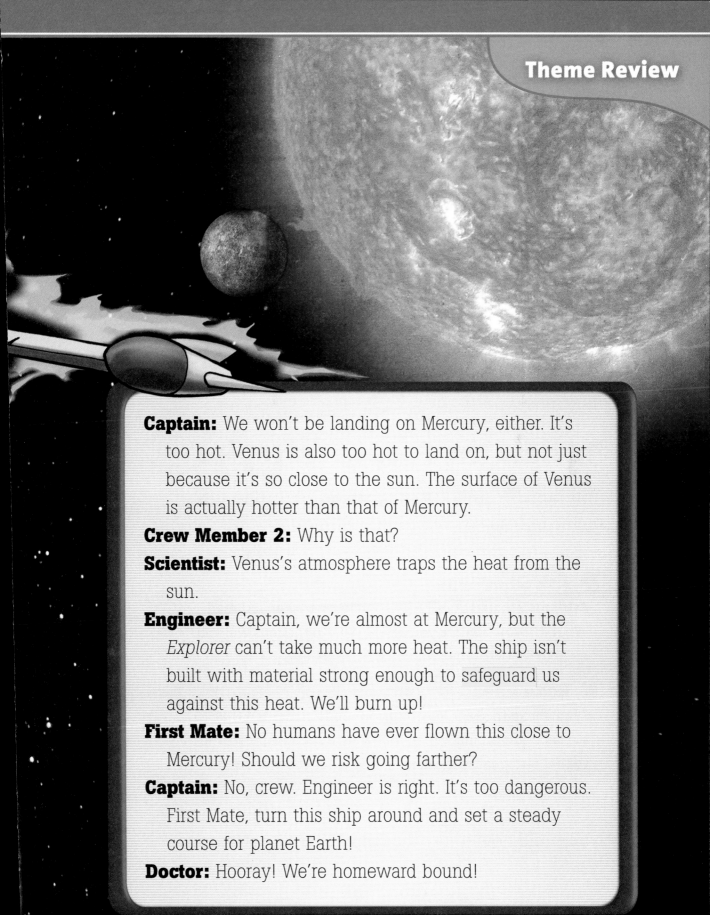

Captain: We won't be landing on Mercury, either. It's too hot. Venus is also too hot to land on, but not just because it's so close to the sun. The surface of Venus is actually hotter than that of Mercury.

Crew Member 2: Why is that?

Scientist: Venus's atmosphere traps the heat from the sun.

Engineer: Captain, we're almost at Mercury, but the *Explorer* can't take much more heat. The ship isn't built with material strong enough to safeguard us against this heat. We'll burn up!

First Mate: No humans have ever flown this close to Mercury! Should we risk going farther?

Captain: No, crew. Engineer is right. It's too dangerous. First Mate, turn this ship around and set a steady course for planet Earth!

Doctor: Hooray! We're homeward bound!

COMPREHENSION STRATEGIES
Review

Reading Functional Text

Bridge to Reading for Information Functional text is writing that is used by people every day. It is text that helps people answer questions and complete tasks. It can be found on a cereal box, in the newspaper, and in a telephone book.

Read the notes on page 425. How can the information help you read different kinds of functional text?

Review the Focus Strategies

You can also use the strategies you learned in this theme to help you read functional text.

Ask Questions

Ask yourself questions before, while, and after you read. What information are you after? What directions will you need to follow? What will the outcome be?

Read Ahead

Read ahead to see if new information is presented that explains something. When following directions, read ahead to find out what you will need and what you will do.

As you read "Energy" on pages 426–427, think about where and how to use the comprehension strategies.

GUIDE WORDS
This article is from an encyclopedia. Guide words are the first words on the page. These words help readers locate information quickly.

DIRECTIONS
Directions for doing or making something are a kind of functional text. Use the numbers and art to help you follow the steps in order.

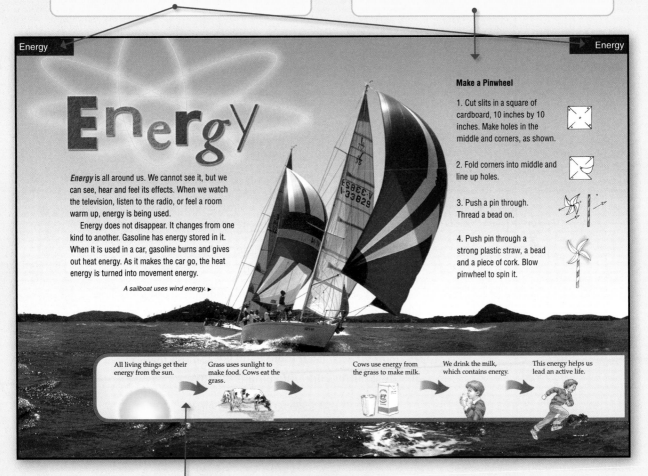

Energy

Energy

Energy

Energy is all around us. We cannot see it, but we can see, hear and feel its effects. When we watch the television, listen to the radio, or feel a room warm up, energy is being used.

Energy does not disappear. It changes from one kind to another. Gasoline has energy stored in it. When it is used in a car, gasoline burns and gives out heat energy. As it makes the car go, the heat energy is turned into movement energy.

A sailboat uses wind energy. ▶

Make a Pinwheel

1. Cut slits in a square of cardboard, 10 inches by 10 inches. Make holes in the middle and corners, as shown.

2. Fold corners into middle and line up holes.

3. Push a pin through. Thread a bead on.

4. Push pin through a strong plastic straw, a bead and a piece of cork. Blow pinwheel to spin it.

All living things get their energy from the sun.

Grass uses sunlight to make food. Cows eat the grass.

Cows use energy from the grass to make milk.

We drink the milk, which contains energy.

This energy helps us lead an active life.

GRAPHIC AIDS
Graphic aids such as maps, diagrams, and flow charts can also help you understand information quickly.

Apply the Strategies Read these pages from an encyclopedia. As you read, stop and think about how you are using comprehension strategies.

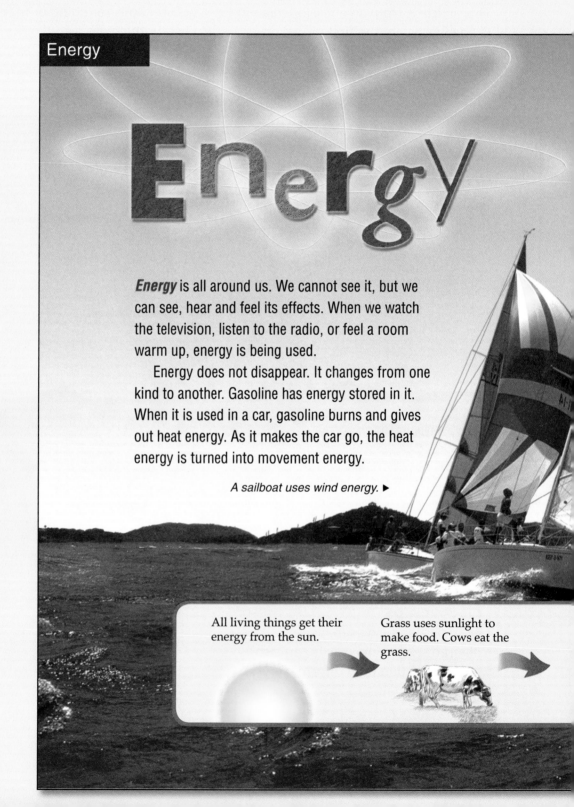

Energy

Energy

Energy is all around us. We cannot see it, but we can see, hear and feel its effects. When we watch the television, listen to the radio, or feel a room warm up, energy is being used.

Energy does not disappear. It changes from one kind to another. Gasoline has energy stored in it. When it is used in a car, gasoline burns and gives out heat energy. As it makes the car go, the heat energy is turned into movement energy.

A sailboat uses wind energy. ▶

All living things get their energy from the sun.

Grass uses sunlight to make food. Cows eat the grass.

Stop and Think

What **questions** do you have as you read? How can **reading ahead** help you answer them?

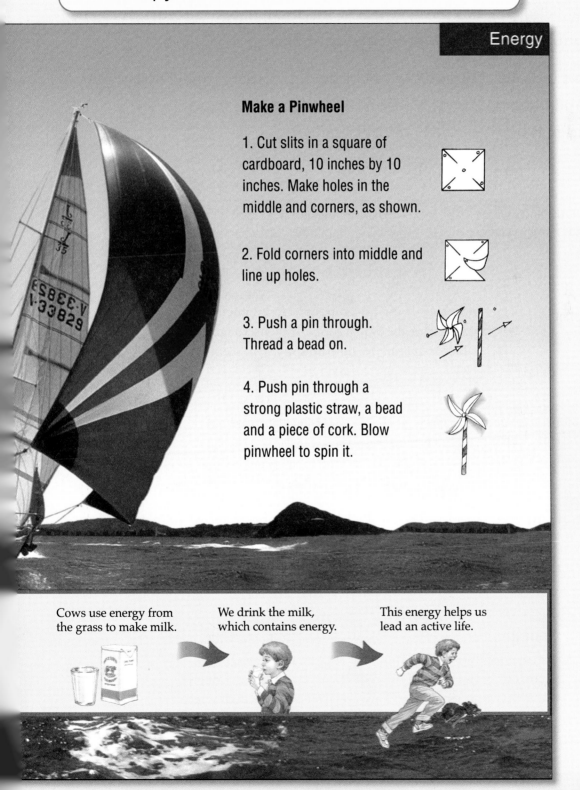

Energy

Make a Pinwheel

1. Cut slits in a square of cardboard, 10 inches by 10 inches. Make holes in the middle and corners, as shown.

2. Fold corners into middle and line up holes.

3. Push a pin through. Thread a bead on.

4. Push pin through a strong plastic straw, a bead and a piece of cork. Blow pinwheel to spin it.

Cows use energy from the grass to make milk.

We drink the milk, which contains energy.

This energy helps us lead an active life.

Using the Glossary

Like a dictionary, this glossary lists words in alphabetical order. To find a word, look it up by its first letter or letters.

To save time, use the guide words at the top of each page. These show the first and last words on the page. Look at the guide words to see if your word falls between them alphabetically.

Here is an example of a glossary entry:

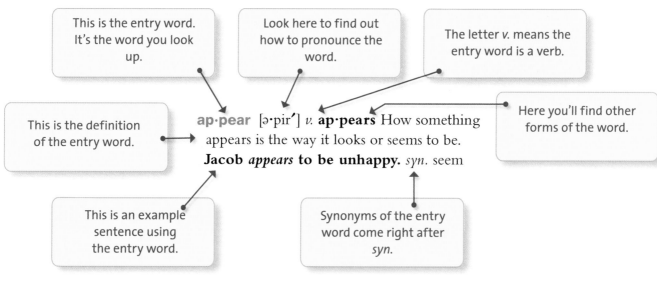

This is the entry word. It's the word you look up.

Look here to find out how to pronounce the word.

The letter v. means the entry word is a verb.

This is the definition of the entry word.

ap·pear [ə·pir'] *v.* **ap·pears** How something appears is the way it looks or seems to be. **Jacob *appears* to be unhappy.** *syn.* seem

Here you'll find other forms of the word.

This is an example sentence using the entry word.

Synonyms of the entry word come right after *syn.*

Word Origins

Throughout the glossary, you will find notes about word origins, or how words got started and have changed. Words often have interesting backgrounds that can help you remember what they mean.

> ── **Word Origins** ──
>
> **dialogue** *Dialogue* means "conversation." To begin with, it came from the Greek word *diálogos.* The prefix *dia-* means "across or between," and the root *légein* means "speak." So, to speak between people is to have a conversation or dialogue.

Pronunciation

The pronunciations in brackets are respellings that show how the words are pronounced.

The pronunciation key explains what the symbols in a respelling mean. A shortened pronunciation key appears on every other page of the glossary.

PRONUNCIATION KEY

a	add, map	m	move, seem	u	up, done
ā	ace, rate	n	nice, tin	û(r)	burn, term
â(r)	care, air	ng	ring, song	yōō	fuse, few
ä	palm, father	o	odd, hot	v	vain, eve
b	bat, rub	ō	open, so	w	win, away
ch	check, catch	ô	order, jaw	y	yet, yearn
d	dog, rod	oi	oil, boy	z	zest, muse
e	end, pet	ou	pout, now	zh	vision, pleasure
ē	equal, tree	ŏŏ	took, full	ə	the schwa, an
f	fit, half	ōō	pool, food		unstressed vowel
g	go, log	p	pit, stop		representing the
h	hope, hat	r	run, poor		sound spelled
i	it, give	s	see, pass		*a* in *above*
ī	ice, write	sh	sure, rush		*e* in *sicken*
j	joy, ledge	t	talk, sit		*i* in *possible*
k	cool, take	th	thin, both		*o* in *melon*
l	look, rule	th	this, bathe		*u* in *circus*

Other symbols:
- • separates words into syllables
- ′ indicates heavier stress on a syllable
- ‚ indicates lighter stress on a syllable

Abbreviations: *adj.* adjective, *adv.* adverb, *conj.* conjunction, *interj.* interjection, *n.* noun, *prep.* preposition, *pron.* pronoun, *syn.* synonym, *v.* verb

A

ab·sence [ab′səns] *n.* Absence means that something or someone is not present. **There was an *absence* of fresh water on the island.** *syn.* lack

ACADEMIC LANGUAGE

accuracy When you read with *accuracy,* you read without any mistakes.

advertisement An *advertisement* is written to sell a product or tell about an event.

a·maze·ment [ə·māz′mənt] *n.* Amazement is a feeling of great wonder and surprise. **When Destinee's baby brother said his first words, she gasped in *amazement*.** *syn.* surprise

am·ple [am′pəl] *adj.* An amount that is ample is enough or more than is needed. **The boys had *ample* space to play football in the yard.** *syns.* enough, plenty

ap·pear [ə·pir′] *v.* **ap·pears** How something appears is the way it looks or seems to be. **Jacob *appears* to be unhappy.** *syn.* seem

B

beck·on [bek′ən] *v.* **beck·oned** If you beckoned to someone, you used your hand to signal him or her to come to you. **Alyssa *beckoned* to Daisy to come over to her desk.** *syn.* summon

boast [bōst] *v.* **boast·ing** Someone who is boasting is telling other people wonderful things about himself or herself. **Joseph was always *boasting* about how fast he could run.** *syn.* brag

brit·tle [brit′əl] *adj.* Things that are brittle are so stiff and hard that they break easily. **A glass vase can be easily broken because it is *brittle*.** *syns.* fragile, breakable

bur·den [bûr′dən] *n.* A burden is a heavy load that is difficult to carry. **For Sierra, the stack of books was a heavy *burden*.**

C

clut·ter [klut′ər] *n.* If a place such as your desk or your room has clutter, it is messy and full of things you do not really need. **The floor of the playroom was covered with *clutter*.**

con·firm [kən·fûrm′] *v.* When you can prove something is correct, you can confirm it. **The cashier called the store manager to *confirm* the price of the bananas.** *syn.* verify

con·sole [kən·sōl′] *v.* When you comfort or cheer someone, you console him or her. **My friends tried to *console* me after I lost the race.** *syn.* encourage

creep [krēp] *v.* **crept** If you crept, you moved slowly and carefully so that you wouldn't be seen or heard. **The cat *crept* up behind the mouse.** *syn.* sneak

creep

crit·i·cize [krit′ə·sīz′] *v.* When you criticize something, you tell what you think is wrong with it. **Sergio was glad that the art teacher did not *criticize* his painting.**

cun·ning [kun′ing] *adj.* Someone who is cunning uses smart and tricky ways to get what he or she wants. **The *cunning* fox crept into the chicken house after dark.** *syns.* sly, crafty

D

de·cent [dē′sənt] *adj.* Someone who is decent is good and fair. **Cameron is a *decent* person who always treats his customers honestly.** *syns.* kind, respectable

de·lib·er·a·tion [di·lib′ə·rā′shən] *n.* Deliberation is thought and discussion that comes before making a decision. **After much *deliberation*, the judges gave the award to Jordan.** *syns.* consideration, thought

de·light·ed [di·līt′id] *adj.* When you are very happy about something, you are delighted. **Sofia was *delighted* when she got an A on her test.** *syns.* overjoyed, thrilled

delighted

de·tail [dē′tāl] *n.* A detail is a small piece of information that is part of a larger whole. **Jada planned every *detail* of her party.**

di·a·logue [dī′ə·lôg′] *n.* Conversation between people is called dialogue. **The two actors had a lot of *dialogue* to memorize for the play.**

— **Word Origins** —

dialogue *Dialogue* means "conversation." To begin with, it came from the Greek word *diálogos*. The prefix *dia-* means "across or between," and the root *légein* means "speak." So, to speak between people is to have a conversation or dialogue.

dim [dim] *adj.* It is dim when there is not much light. **The *dim* light of the room made it difficult for Leslie to read.**

dis·grace·ful [dis·grās′fəl] *adj.* If something is disgraceful, it is shocking and not acceptable. **James thought his poor performance in the game was *disgraceful*.** *syns.* dreadful, shameful

dis·guise [dis·gīz′] *v.* **dis·guised** If you are disguised, you are wearing something that keeps people from knowing who you are. **Maya was *disguised* by a mask when she came to the costume party.** *syn.* camouflage

disguise

a	add	e	end	o	odd	o͞o	pool	oi	oil	th	this	zh	vision
ā	ace	ē	equal	ō	open	u	up	ou	pout	zh	vision		
â	care	i	it	ô	order	û	burn	ng	ring				
ä	palm	ī	ice	o͝o	took	yo͞o	fuse	th	thin				

ə = { *a* in *above*, *e* in *sicken*, *i* in *possible*, *o* in *melon*, *u* in *circus* }

doze [dōz] *v.* **doz·es** Someone who dozes takes short naps. **The baby usually** *dozes* **in her crib after she eats.** *syns.* sleep, snooze

drift [drift] *v.* **drifts** When something drifts, it moves along without direction. **Mikayla watches as the boat** *drifts* **down the stream.** *syn.* float

drow·sy [drou′zē] *adj.* When you are drowsy, you feel so sleepy that you can't stay awake. **Although Andrew got plenty of sleep, he still felt** *drowsy*. *syns.* sleepy, tired

E

ef·fort [ef′ərt] *n.* When you work hard, you use effort. **It took a lot of** *effort* **to clean up the playground after the storm.** *syn.* work

ACADEMIC LANGUAGE

e-mail An *e-mail* is a written message sent from one computer to another.

em·brace [im·brās′] *v.* **em·braced** If you hugged someone, you embraced that person. **Angela** *embraced* **her grandmother as soon as she walked through the door.** *syns.* hug, squeeze

embrace

e·mo·tion [i·mō′shən] *n.* An emotion is a feeling, such as happiness. **Michael was filled with** *emotion* **when he found out that the book had belonged to his great-grandfather.** *syn.* feeling

e·nor·mous [i′nôr′məs] *adj.* Something that is enormous is very big. **The elephant's footprints were** *enormous*. *syns.* huge, gigantic

e·rupt [i·rupt′] *v.* Something that erupts breaks out of something that holds it. **Lava will** *erupt* **when the pressure inside the volcano becomes too great.**

— **Word Origins** —

erupt This word is borrowed from the Latin word *ēruptus* or *ērumpere*, which means "to break out or burst forth."

ev·i·dence [ev′ə·dəns] *n.* Evidence is proof that something has happened. **The footprints were** *evidence* **that deer had been in the yard.** *syns.* proof, confirmation

ex·claim [iks·klām′] *v.* **ex·claimed** If you exclaimed something, you said it excitedly. **"I can't believe we won!" Elizabeth** *exclaimed*.

ex·pand [ik·spand′] *v.* When things expand, they get bigger. **We watched the balloon** *expand* **as the air filled it.** *syn.* swell

expand

flus·ter [flus′tər] *v.* **flus·tered** If something flustered you, it made you forget what you were saying or doing. **It *flustered* Oscar to have so many people watching him.** *syns.* distract, confuse

flut·ter [flut′ər] *v.* **flut·ter·ing** When something moves through the air lightly and quickly, it is fluttering. **The moth's wings were *fluttering* as it flew around the light.** *syn.* flap

fondness [fond′nəs] *n.* If you like something very much, you have a fondness for it. **Hayley has a *fondness* for fresh pineapple.** *syns.* weakness, affection

func·tion·al [fungk′shən·əl] *adj.* Something that serves a purpose is functional. **The birthday gift, a sweater, was both pretty and *functional*.** *syn.* practical

gen·er·ate [jen′ə·rāt′] *v.* **gen·er·ates** To generate something is to produce it. **We bought a machine that *generates* electricity.** *syn.* produce

glance [glans] *v.* **glanc·ing** When you are glancing at something, you are taking a quick look at it. **Tyler kept *glancing* at the clock to see how much time was left.** *syns.* look, glimpse

glo·ri·ous [glôr′ē·əs] *adj.* If something is so wonderful that you can hardly believe it, it is glorious. **The cake was a *glorious* surprise for Jackson's birthday.** *syns.* wonderful, splendid

grain·y [grā′nē] *adj.* If something is grainy, it is not smooth but has many small, hard pieces. **When Donald mixed the paint with sand, it felt *grainy*.** *syn.* gritty

a	add	e	end	o	odd	o͞o	pool	oi	oil	th	this		a in *above*
ā	ace	ē	equal	ō	open	u	up	ou	pout	zh	vision		e in *sicken*
â	care	i	it	ô	order	û	burn	ng	ring			ə =	i in *possible*
ä	palm	ī	ice	o͝o	took	yo͞o	fuse	th	thin				o in *melon*
													u in *circus*

he·ro·ic [hi·rō′ik] *adj.* Someone who is heroic is brave and acts like a hero. **The mayor thanked the firefighter for her** *heroic* **act.** *syns.* courageous, brave

ACADEMIC LANGUAGE

historical fiction *Historical fiction* is a made-up story that is set in the past with people, places, and events that did happen or could have happened.

how-to article A *how-to article* gives step-by-step instructions for completing a task or project.

im·merse [i·mûrs′] *v.* To immerse oneself is to become very involved in something. **Alexis would** *immerse* **herself in any book she was reading.** *syn.* sink

ACADEMIC LANGUAGE

informational narrative *Informational narrative* presents information in the form of a story.

in·hab·i·tant [in·hab′ə·tənt] *n.* **in·hab·i·tants** The people or animals that live in a certain place are the inhabitants of that place. **Two little goldfish were the only** *inhabitants* **of the fishbowl.** *syn.* occupant

in·her·it [in·her′it] *v.* When you inherit something, you have been given something by someone who used to own it. **Brittany will** *inherit* **her sister's bicycle when her sister grows too tall for it.**

ACADEMIC LANGUAGE

interview An *interview* is a conversation in which one person asks questions and another person gives answers.

intonation *Intonation* is the rise and fall of your voice as you read aloud.

ACADEMIC LANGUAGE

magazine article A *magazine article* is a short selection that appears in a magazine and gives information about a topic.

mag·ni·fy [mag′nə·fī′] *v.* When you magnify something, you make it look larger than it actually is. **Noah used the microscope to** *magnify* **the surface of the leaf.** *syn.* enlarge

man·da·to·ry [man′də·tôr′ē] *adj.* Something that is mandatory is required. **Mr. Greene said that writing the book report is** *mandatory*. *syns.* necessary, required

mem·o·ry [mem′ər·ē] *n.* A memory is something you remember. **Maria's favorite** *memory* **was the day her dad brought home a new puppy.** *syn.* remembrance

men·tion [men′shən] *v.* **men·tioned** If you mentioned something, you talked about it briefly. **David *mentioned* wanting to be the first to try the new computer game.** *syns.* say, remark

ACADEMIC LANGUAGE

myth A *myth* is a story that shows what a group of people in the past believed about how something came to be.

noc·tur·nal [nok·tûr′nəl] *adj.* An animal that is nocturnal sleeps during the day and is active at night. **Raccoons and opossums are active at night because they are *nocturnal* animals.**

— Word Origins —

nocturnal The Latin word *nox* means "night," and *nocturnes* means "belonging to the night."

nui·sance [noo′səns] *n.* Something or someone that bothers you can be a nuisance. **The neighbor's barking dog was a *nuisance*.** *syns.* pest, irritation

o·blige [ə·blīj′] *v.* When you oblige someone, you help the person. **Austin is always happy to *oblige* when anyone needs help spelling a word.** *syns.* help, assist

ob·serve [əb·zûrv′] *v.* **ob·served** If you observed something, you watched it carefully to learn more about it. **Elijah *observed* the tree's changes in each season.** *syns.* study, examine

o·ver·hear [ō′vər·hir′] *v.* **o·ver·heard** If you overheard what people said, you heard it without their knowing that you were listening. **Amir *overheard* his sister talking on the phone.**

ACADEMIC LANGUAGE

pace Reading at an appropriate *pace* means reading at the right speed.

per·ma·nent [pûr′mən·ənt] *adj.* **per·ma·nent·ly** If something stays one way forever, it stays that way permanently. **The statue was set in the ground *permanently* so that it could not be moved.**

ACADEMIC LANGUAGE

phrasing *Phrasing* is the grouping of words into small "chunks," or phrases, when you read aloud.

pic·tur·esque [pik′chə·resk′] *adj.* Something that is picturesque is pretty enough to be in a picture. **The old village with its colorful flowers and little cottages was *picturesque*.** *syn.* charming

a	add	e	end	o	odd	o͞o	pool	oi	oil	th	this		a in *above*
ā	ace	ē	equal	ō	open	u	up	ou	pout	zh	vision		e in *sicken*
â	care	i	it	ô	order	û	burn	ng	ring			ə = {	i in *possible*
ä	palm	ī	ice	o͝o	took	yo͞o	fuse	th	thin				o in *melon*
													u in *circus*

play A *play* is a story written so that it can be performed for an audience.

poetry *Poetry* uses rhythm and imagination to express feelings and ideas.

prey [prā] *n.* An animal that is hunted for food is prey. **The zebra became *prey* for a hungry lion.**

punctuation Paying attention to *punctuation* will help you read a text correctly.

R

reading rate Your *reading rate* is how quickly you can read a text correctly and still understand what you are reading.

realistic fiction *Realistic fiction* is a story that could happen in real life.

reel [rēl] *v.* **reels 1.** A person reels something in by winding up a line attached to it. **Brian watches as Grandma *reels* in a big fish.** *syn.* pull **2.** When a person reels, he or she feels dizzy and sways from side to side. **Kevin *reels* after stepping off a carousel.** *syns.* sway, stagger

re·flect [ri·flekt′] *v.* **re·flects 1.** When something reflects light, the light bounces off the surface instead of passing through it. **A mirror *reflects* an image of whatever is in front of it. 2.** When someone reflects, he or she thinks about something that happened in the past. **Ryan *reflects* on what he has learned and then writes about it in his journal.**

reflect

re·hearse [ri·hûrs′] *v.* To rehearse is to practice for a performance. **Jasmine wanted to *rehearse* her lines for the play.** *syn.* practice

re·mark [ri·märk′] *n.* A remark is something that is said about something. **Karen was pleased with the kind *remark* Ms. Hill had written on her paper.** *syns.* comment, statement

re·quire [ri·kwīr′] *v.* **re·quired** Something that is required is needed. **Each member of the baseball team is *required* to attend all the practices.**

re·spon·si·bil·i·ty [ri·spon′sə·bil′ə·tē] *n.* A responsibility is something you are expected to do. **It was Trevor's *responsibility* to collect the tennis rackets after the game.** *syns.* duty, job

ri·dic·u·lous [ri·dik′yə·ləs] *adj.* Something that is very silly is ridiculous. **Brandon laughed at the *ridiculous* joke his mom told him.**

ro·tate [rō′tāt] *v.* **ro·tates** Something that rotates spins like a top. **Earth *rotates* on its axis once every 24 hours.**

ru·in [roō′in] *v.* **ru·ined** If something is ruined, it is no longer any good. **Devin's shirt was *ruined* when he accidentally spilled paint on it.** *syn.* spoil

S

safe·guard [sāf′gärd′] *v.* To safeguard something is to protect and guard it. **Emily brought the potted plant indoors to *safeguard* it from the cold.** *syn.* protect

scarce [skârs] *adj.* Something is scarce if there is not much of it to be found. **Open land is *scarce* in the crowded city.** *syn.* rare

ACADEMIC LANGUAGE

science fiction *Science fiction* is a made-up story set in the future with ideas from science.

scold [skōld] *v.* **scold·ing** If you are scolding someone, you are angrily pointing out that person's mistakes. **The mother is *scolding* her child for misbehaving.**

sed·en·tar·y [sed′ən·târ′ē] *adj.* If you have a sedentary job or lifestyle, you are sitting down most of the time. **The hen has become *sedentary* since she laid her eggs.** *syn.* inactive

shal·low [shal′ō] *adj.* Something shallow is not very deep. **Stay in the *shallow* end of the pool.**

shel·ter [shel′tər] *v.* **shel·ters** Something that shelters you protects you and keeps you safe. **The tree's shade *shelters* us from the sun.** *syns.* protect, cover

so·cial [sō′shəl] *adj.* A social animal is one that lives in a group with other animals of the same kind. **Monkeys are *social* animals that share the care of their young.**

spi·ral [spī′rəl] *adj.* A spiral shape curls around and around in a circle. **The tornado looked like a *spiral* cloud.** *syns.* twisted, coiled

— **Word Origins** —

spiral The Latin *spiralis* means "to wind, coil, or twist." Today, the English *spiral* still has the same meaning.

sprin·kle [spring′kəl] *v.* **sprin·kled** Something that has been sprinkled has had tiny pieces or drops of something scattered all over it. **The blue floor that we had *sprinkled* with yellow paint was very colorful.**

stead·y [sted′ē] *adj.* A light that is steady always looks the same and does not change or go out. **The *steady* beam of the flashlight clearly showed the raccoon.** *syn.* continuous

a	add	e	end	o	odd	oō	pool	oi	oil	th	this		ə =	*a* in *above*
ā	ace	ē	equal	ō	open	u	up	ou	pout	zh	vision			*e* in *sicken*
â	care	i	it	ô	order	û	burn	ng	ring					*i* in *possible*
ä	palm	ī	ice	oō	took	yoō	fuse	th	thin					*o* in *melon*
														u in *circus*

strand [strand] *n.* **strands** Long, thin pieces of something are strands. **It is difficult to see the *strands* of a spiderweb.** *syn.* string

streak [strēk] *v.* To streak is to move very quickly from one place to another. **A falling star will *streak* across the sky.** *syns.* zoom, flash

sug·gest [səg·jest'] *v.* **sug·gest·ed** If you suggested something, you gave someone an idea. **Ethan *suggested* that we finish our homework before dinner.** *syn.* recommend

sum·mon [sum'ən] *v.* **sum·mon·ing** If you are summoning someone, you are calling for the person to come. **Vanessa was *summoning* her brother to the table.** *syns.* beckon, call

sur·face [sûr'fis] *n.* The surface of something is the top part of it. **Dolphins must come up to the *surface* of the water to breathe.**

Word Origins

surface What does your face have to do with the word *surface*? *Surface* was originally a French word. The prefix *sur-* means "above," and *face* means "face." So, since a face is what we see as the front and top of something, a surface is the top or outer part of something.

---

sway [swā] *v.* When things sway, they swing slowly back and forth. **The branches *sway* back and forth in the breeze.** *syn.* swing

swift [swift] *adj.* Something that is swift moves very quickly. **The *swift* runner finished the race quickly.** *syns.* fast, rapid

swoop [swoop] *v.* **swoops** When something swoops, it dives or dips downward. **The pelican *swoops* toward the water to catch a fish.** *syns.* dive, plunge

swoop

ACADEMIC LANGUAGE

syllable A *syllable* is the smallest part of a word that contains a single vowel sound.

ten·der [ten'dər] *adj.* Something, like food, that is tender is soft and easy to chew or cut. **The meat was *tender* and juicy.**

ACADEMIC LANGUAGE

textbook A *textbook* is a book that is used in schools to teach a subject.

thor·ough [thûr'ō] *adj.* If you do something in a thorough way, you do a careful and complete job. **James gave his room a *thorough* cleaning.** *syns.* complete, careful

ACADEMIC LANGUAGE

travel journal A *travel journal* is a personal record of events that happen while going from one place to another.

V

vain [vān] *adj.* If you are vain, you think very highly of yourself. **The *vain* boy spent a lot of time thinking about how handsome he was.** *syns.* conceited, arrogant

ver·sion [vûr′zhən] *n.* **ver·sions** If there are different versions of a story, the story is told in different ways. **Sean wondered if the second *version* of his short story was better than the first.**

--- **Word Origins** ---

version The word *version* comes from the Latin *versionem,* which means "a turning." So when you hear a new version of a story, it has made a turn and is told in another way.

vis·i·ble [viz′ə·bəl] a*dj.* When something is visible, you can see it. **The fireworks were *visible* for miles around.** *syn.* noticeable

visible

Y

yank [yangk] *v.* **yanked** If you yanked something, you gave it a quick, hard pull. **The man *yanked* on the cord to start the boat's motor.** *syns.* tug, pull

a	add	e	end	o	odd	o͞o	pool	oi	oil	th	this		a in *above*
ā	ace	ē	equal	ō	open	u	up	ou	pout	zh	vision		e in *sicken*
â	care	i	it	ô	order	û	burn	ng	ring			ə =	i in *possible*
ä	palm	ī	ice	o͝o	took	yo͞o	fuse	th	thin				o in *melon*
													u in *circus*

439

Index of Titles and Authors

Page numbers in green refer to biographical information.

Acknowledgments

For permission to reprint copyrighted material, grateful acknowledgment is made to the following sources:

Bayard Presse Canada Inc.: From "Bottlenose Dolphins" in *chickaDEE* Magazine, April 1999.

Candlewick Press, Inc., Cambridge, MA From "The Science Fair" in *Beany and the Meany* by Susan Wojciechowski, illustrated by Susanna Natti. Text copyright © 2005 by Susan Wojciechowski; illustrations copyright © 2005 by Susanna Natti.

Candlewick Press, Inc., Cambridge, MA, on behalf of Walker Books Ltd., London: From *Bat Loves the Night* by Nicola Davies, illustrated by Sarah Fox-Davies. Text copyright © 2001 by Nicola Davies; illustrations copyright © 2001 by Sarah Fox-Davies.

Chelsea House Publishers: From "The life cycle of moths and butterflies" (Retitled: "Caterpillars Spin Webs Too!") in *Insects and Spiders: Moths and butterflies* by Shane F. McEvey, for the Australian Museum. Text copyright © 2001 by the Australian Museum Trust.

The Cricket Magazine Group, a division of Carus Publishing Company: "The Cracked Chinese Jug" by Carolyn Han, illustrated by Christine Joy Pratt from *Spider* Magazine, July 2003. Text copyright © 2003 by Carolyn Han; illustrations copyright © by Christine Joy Pratt.

Dell Publishing, a division of Random House, Inc.: *Half-Chicken/Mediopollito* by Alma Flor Ada, illustrated by Kim Howard. Text copyright © 1995 by Alma Flor Ada; illustrations copyright © 1995 by Kim Howard.

Dial Books for Young Readers, a Division of Penguin Young Readers Group, A Member of Penguin Group (USA) Inc., 345 Hudson St., New York, NY 10014: From *Me and Uncle Romie: A Story Inspired by the Life and Art of Romare Bearden* by Claire Hartfield, illustrated by Jerome Lagarrigue. Text copyright © 2002 by Claire Hartfield; illustrations copyright © 2002 by Jerome Lagarrigue.

Harcourt, Inc.: Untitled poem (Titled: "For You") from *Oddhopper Opera: A Bug's Garden of Verses* by Kurt Cyrus. Copyright © 2001 by Kurt Cyrus. "Diary of a Very Short Winter Day" from *Antarctic Antics: A Book of Penguin Poems* by Judy Sierra, illustrated by Jose Aruego and Ariane Dewey. Text copyright © 1998 by Judy Sierra; illustrations copyright © 1998 by Jose Aruego and Ariane Dewey.

HarperCollins Publishers: From *Ramona Quimby, Age 8* by Beverly Cleary, cover illustration by Alan Tiegreen. Text and cover illustration copyright © 1981 by Beverly Cleary. "I Sailed on Half a Ship" from *a Pizza the size of the Sun* by Jack Prelutsky. Text copyright © 1994, 1996 by Jack Prelutsky. From *Charlotte's Web* by E. B. White, illustrated by Garth Williams. Copyright 1952 by E. B. White; text copyright © renewed 1980 by E. B. White; illustrations copyright © renewed 1980 by Estate of Garth Williams.

Holiday House, Inc.: Adapted from *The Planets* by Gail Gibbons. Copyright © 1993, 2005 by Gail Gibbons.

Henry Holt and Company, LLC: *Antarctic Ice* by Jim Mastro and Norbert Wu, photographs by Norbert Wu. Text copyright © 2003 by Jim Mastro and Norbert Wu; photographs copyright © 2003 by Norbert Wu.

Houghton Mifflin Company: From *Chestnut Cove* by Tim Egan. Copyright © 1995 by Tim Egan. "Energy" from *The Kingfisher Young World Encyclopedia.* Text copyright © 1994 by Larousse plc.

Lee & Low Books Inc., New York, 10016: "Abuelita's Lap" from *Confetti: Poems for Children* by Pat Mora, cover illustration by Enrique O. Sanchez. Text copyright © 1996 by Pat Mora; cover illustration copyright © 1996 by Enrique O. Sanchez.

Lerner Publications: From *Mayors* by Shannon Knudsen, photographs by Stephen G. Donaldson. Text copyright © 2006 by Lerner Publications Company; photographs copyright © 2006 by Stephen G. Donaldson.

National Geographic Society: From *Spiders and Their Webs* by Darlyne A. Murawski, illustrated by Mark Burrier. Copyright © 2004 by Darlyne A. Murawski.

Philomel Books, a Division of Penguin Young Reader's Group, A Member of Penguin Group (USA) Inc., 345 Hudson St., New York, NY 10014: Lon Po Po: A Red-Riding Hood Story from China, translated and illustrated by Ed Young, cover calligraphy by John Stevens. Copyright © 1989 by Ed Young; cover calligraphy copyright © 1989 by John Stevens.

Lois Simmie: From "Jeremy's House" in *Auntie's Knitting a Baby* by Lois Simmie. Text copyright © 1984 by Lois Simmie.

Photo Credits

Placement Key: (t) top; (b) bottom; (l) left; (r) right; (c) center; (bg) background; (fg) foreground; (i) inset

16 (b) PhotoDisc; 17 (cr) PhotoDisc; 37 (br) Tom Sobolik / Black Star; 42 Rick Orrell/shutterstock; 48 (bl) James L. Amos/Corbis; 51 (cr) NORBERT WU /Minden Pictures; 72 (br) David Toerge / Black Star; 73 (bl) Henry Feather / Black Star; 85 (cr) Morgan and Marvin Smith/Monica Smith (copyright holder) and Photographs and Prints Division, Schomburg center for Research in Black Culture, the New York Public Library, Astor, Lenox, and Tilden Foundations; 86 (bl) Art Resource; 87 (tr) Art Resource; (cr) Chester Higgins, Jr.; 108 (bl) Larry Evans / Black Star; 109 (br) Courtesy Jerome LaGarrigue; 110 (cr) Mike Maloney / Black Star; 111 (tr) © Martin Heitner / SuperStock; 112 (t) Telescope; 115 (bl) Royalty-Free/Corbis; 116 (t) Jason Cheever; RF/Shutterstock; 117 (tr) Ingram; 119 (tr) © BAUMANN, PETER / Animals Animals/ Earth Scenes All rights reserved; 137 (br) Kirsten Shultz; 140 (t) Chow Shue Ma; RF/Shutterstock; 141 (tr) Photodisc Green/Getty Images; 156 © 2007 Artists Rights Society, NY/Erich Lessing / Art Resource, NY; 158 Raldi Somers; RF/Shutterstock; 160 (bl) John Parker/Getty Images; 161 (tr) Corbis; 162 (bl) Getty; 163 (tr) Corbis; 165-182 Norbert Wu norbertwu.com; 184 (bc) Michael J. Maloney / Black Star; 185 © 2006 Peter Brueggeman, www. norbertwu.com; 196 (bl) David A. Northcott/Corbis; 197 (tr) David A. Northcott/Corbis; 198 (bc) Edgar T. Jones/Bruce Coleman USA; 199 (tr) J.S. Dunning/Bruce Coleman USA; 216 (tr) Michael St Maur Sheil / Black Star; 221 (tr) Getty Images RF; 249 (br) Kieth Skelton/ Black Star; 253 (tr) foodfolio/Alamy Images; 255 (br) Larry Williams/Corbis; 256 (cr) Getty; 257 (cr) Dorling Kindersley/Getty; 273 (tr) Alan McEwen; 274 © Grace/zefa/Corbis; 275 (c) Mitchell Layton/Duomo/CORBIS; 276 (t) PhotoCreate; RF/Shutterstock; 292 SuperStock Rights Managed; 295 (bl) Digital Stock, Corbis Corporation; 296 (bl) Amy Ford/shutterstock; 297 (cr) OSF/ MANTIS W.F. / Animals Animals - Earth Scenes; 298 (br) Ingram; 298 (t) Rustam Burganov; RF/Shutterstock; 299 (tr) Bogdan Postelnicu/Shutterstock; 312 (br) Louis Fabian Bachrach; 314 Marco Regalia; RF/Shutterstock; 315 (tr) Creativ Studio Heinem/age fotostock; 315 (br) Svetlana Larina/shutterstock; 317 (tr) PhotoDisc; 324 (bl) Digital Vision; 326 (t) Mike Brake/Shutterstock; 326 (bl) LESZCZYNSKI, ZIGMUND / Animals Animals - Earth Scenes; 345 (br) Mike Maloney / Black Star; 354 (bl) PhotoDisc, Inc.; 355 (tr) StockFood Creative; 374 (bl) © Royalty-Free/Corbis; 375 (bl) David Michael Zimmerman/Corbis; 377 (tr) PhotoDisc; 379 (bl) StockTrek; 381 (cr) NASA; 382 (bl) The Yohkoh Soft X-ray Telescope was a collaborative project of the Lockheed Palo Alto Research Laboratory, the National Astronomical Observatory of Japan, and the University of Tokyo, supported by NASA and ISAS.; 383 (tr) National Geographic; 405 (br) Mike Maloney / Black Star; 409 (tr) StockTrek; 413 Sebastian Kaulitzki/shutterstock; 420 (bl) © Brand X / Imagestate; 420 Geoffrey Clements/Corbis; 423 (tr) Associated Press, NASA.

All other photos © Harcourt School Publishers. Harcourt photos provided by Harcourt Index, Harcourt IPR, and Harcourt Photographers: Weronica Ankarorn, Eric Camden, Doug DuKane, Ken Kinsie, April Riehm and Steve Williams.

Illustration Credits

Cover Art; Laura and Eric Ovresat, Artlab, Inc.